(See page iv for Legend.)

MONOGRAPH 42
AMERICAN ETHNOLOGICAL SOCIETY
JUNE HELM, EDITOR

DAHOMEY
and the

Karl Polanyi

IN COLLABORATION WITH ABRAHAM ROTSTEIN

FOREWORD BY PAUL BOHANNAN

SEATTLE AND LONDON

SLAVE TRADE

An Analysis of an Archaic Economy

UNIVERSITY OF WASHINGTON PRESS

THE ROYAL PALACE

AND THE EUROPEAN FACTORIES AT SAVI (*endpapers*)

Legend

A. Offices of the French *Compagnie des Indes*
B. Hall
C. Director's Residence
D. Assistant Director's Residence
E. Warehouse
G. Servants' Residence
H. French flag
I. Blacksmith
L. Kitchen
M. Outhouse
N. Wine Cellar
O. Vegetable garden
P. Gate to the town
Q. Main gate
R. Large pit from which earth was taken for building purposes
S. Rear courtyard

1. English factory
2. Kitchen
3. Employees' Residence
4. Director's Pavilion
5. English flag

a. The large courtyard of the royal palace and wall
b. Second courtyard
c. Kitchen courtyard
d. Courtyard of the small palace
e. Residence of the servants of the small palace
f. Pavilion where the king and his wives see the populace
g. House of the first valet of the king's bedchamber
h. The king's cannons

aa. Dutch factory
bb. Director's Residence
cc. Employees' Residence
dd. Garden
ee. Lower courtyard and Dutch flag

aaa. Portuguese factory
bbb. Director's Residence
ccc. Employees' Residence
ddd. Lower courtyard
eee. Slaves' Residence
fff. Portuguese flag
hhh. Hut for the Serpent giving birth. As soon as the Negroes see a serpent about to give birth they build similar huts for it even if it is in the street.

Copyright © 1966 by the University of Washington Press
Library of Congress Catalog Card Number 66–19569
Printed in the United States of America

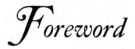# *Foreword*

The death of Karl Polanyi on the twenty-third of April, 1964, when he was seventy-seven years old, brought to a close one of the most productive, quiet working lives in the fields of economic history and economic anthropology, and a scholarly existence that belonged intensely and typically to the twentieth century. Polanyi, for all that some of his later students—impressed with his erudition and disregard for the ordinary—described him as "otherworldly," was at the storm center of the world he lived in.

As a young man, he was founder of the Galilei Society in Budapest, which could be described as the cradle of the liberal revolutions in Hungary in the first decades of our century. For fighting in connection with that organization, he was expelled from the University of Budapest, and ultimately finished his degree in law at Kolozsvár, a Hungarian city and university (the latter since closed) in what is today Rumania. In the first World War, he was a cavalry officer. After that war, ill and as a political refugee, he went to Vienna. There he became a columnist and commentator for the *Oesterreichische Volkswirt,* in charge of analysis of international affairs. For years he read daily *The Times, Le Temps,* the *Frankfurter Zeitung,* all the Vienna papers and those from Budapest and others as they were relevant. When the *Volkswirt* had to forego its liberal tradition in an attempt to stay afloat in the 1930's, Polanyi lost his job and he emigrated to England.

His first trips to America were made during the late 1930's and early 1940's, when he covered most of the states of the union giving background lectures in European history, economy, and current events to college and university audiences.

During his stay in England, Polanyi became a tutor for the Extramural Delagacy of Oxford University and equivalent bodies of the University of London, both of which act in close cooperation with the Workers' Educational Association. There he threw himself into the work of reanalysis of English economic history which was to become *The Great Transformation*.

After World War II, Polanyi came to Columbia University to teach economic history. His influence on students from many of the social sciences and humanities was tremendous; his courses were always popular and well attended. During his last years at Columbia, and during his early years of retirement, Polanyi was joined by Conrad Arensberg in heading a large interdisciplinary project for the comparative study of economic systems. The volume that resulted was *Trade and Market in the Early Empires,* a landmark in economic anthropology and economic history.

Polanyi's interest in Dahomey stems from the years on the "project." One of his students, Rosemary Arnold, had contributed two papers on Dahomey to *Trade and Market.* Polanyi had grown interested and, with characteristic thoroughness, gone completely into the literature on that West African kingdom. The present book, with which he was assisted by Abraham Rotstein, first a graduate student, then a lecturer at the University of Toronto, resulted from these last years of productive scholarship.

Dahomey and the Slave Trade has been carefully prepared for the press by Polanyi's widow, Ilona Duczyńska Polanyi, and with the tireless efforts of June Helm, assisted by Beryl Gillespie. George Dalton has helped with references, and has been invaluable in clearing up meaning in a few places where the manuscript was unclear. Most of the text is, however, as Polanyi wrote it (or, for Chapters Three and Four, as he rewrote Rotstein's drafts). Susan Messerley collated the bibliography from the many sources in which it had been left.

This book is of vital importance to anthropology for several reasons, the most compelling being that the concerns of history and of anthropology are overlapped in it. Besides making available the economic history of one of the great West African kingdoms, it sets forth some new theory for economic anthropology—particularly Part III, in which Polanyi makes sense of the intricacies of trade between a people with a fully monetized economy, and one without, and those passages in which he adds "householding" as a concept to his ideas about the principles of economic integration.

Polanyi's position in economic anthropology—not to mention the status he achieved as economic historian, translator of Hungarian literature, man of action, and inspiring teacher—is secure. He has enabled anthropologists to focus their studies of economy on processes of allocation rather than on processes of production, thereby bringing the studies into line with economic theory without merely "applying" economic theory to systems it was not designed to explain. The "release" that resulted from this great stride forward can be compared, for economic anthropology and studies in comparative economics, with the importance of the discovery in the late nineteenth century of the price mechanism itself. The more we know about the workings of other, and strange, economies, the more we can know of our own. Polanyi's work will stand as a major source of comparative insight—the core of anthropological purpose.

PAUL BOHANNAN

Evanston, Illinois
August, 1965

Preface

The present study is in the field of economic history. For its anthropology, it relies heavily on Melville Herskovits' *Dahomey* (1938). This book was written in collaboration with my close friend Abraham Rotstein, lecturer in economics at the University of Toronto. Edouard Dunglas' more recent account of the history of Ketu (1957–58) served as a key to Rev. S. Johnson's earlier *History of the Yorubas* (1921). Publications of the Institut Français d'Afrique Noire (IFAN) on historic Porto Novo and the Afro-Americans have added to our documentary sources about Dahomey. Historical and, to some extent, economic knowledge on the Niger Bend and on Nigeria are accumulating, likewise thanks to IFAN and its important contributor, Paul Mercier (1951; 1954a, b, c). On the slave trade John Johnston's ship's papers of 1791–92 (1930), Gaston-Martin (1948), Simone Berbain (1942) and K. G. Davies (1957) have supplied unpublished data. Endre Sik's *Histoire de l'Afrique Noire* (1961–63) takes up the theme from the Africans' point of view.

Sources of direct quotations are given in the text. Sources for other assertions are not individually cited in order to avoid overburdening the text with footnotes.

Acknowledgements are due to Mrs. Rosemary Arnold, who delved into the data on the port of trade of eighteenth-century Whydah as research assistant on the Columbia Project on the origins of economic institutions, launched in 1948 with support of the Columbia Council for Research in the Social Sciences. First to offer friendly assistance to my scholarly efforts was Douglas Jolly, M.D., of London, in 1947. From 1953–58 the

ix

Ford Foundation lent its support to the Interdisciplinary Project on the economic aspects of institutional growth carried out at Columbia University. In later years other scholarly bodies assisted me in the following up of the Project which continued to encompass the study of the Dahomean economy from the institutional angle. I wish to express my indebtedness to the Behavioral Science Division of the Ford Foundation, the Wenner-Gren Foundation, the Social Science Research Council, and the American Philosophical Society.

K.P.

Contents

PERSPECTIVE   XV

PART I. THE FRAME OF HISTORY

CHAPTER ONE.   An Inland Dynasty and the Gap
                 of Benin   3

CHAPTER TWO.   The Challenge of the Slave Trade   17

PART II. PATTERNS OF THE ECONOMY

CHAPTER THREE.   Redistribution: The State Sphere   33
                 Annual Customs   33
                 Army   36
                 Economic Administration   37
                 Census   40
                 Taxation   44
                 Royal Equivalents   49
                 The Palace   52
                 Administration and Duality   53

CHAPTER FOUR.   Reciprocity: Mutual Aid
                 and Cooperation   60
                 Work Teams   62
                 Craft Guilds   65
                 Familial Aid   66
                 The Best Friend   67
                 The Pawn   68

CHAPTER FIVE.   Householding: Land and Religion   70
                 Plantation and Peasant Plot   70
                 The Sib and the Compound   70
                 Succession and Inheritance   74
                 Ancestor Worship and Cult House   76
                 The Economic Balance of Religion   79

CHAPTER SIX.   Exchange: Isolated Markets   81
                 No Price-Making Markets   81
                 Compulsory Use of Money   84
                 No Credit, Cash Only   85
                 Retailer's Reward:
                     Double Numeration   85
                 Setting the Prices   87
                 Changing the Set Price   90
                 Cheap Food   91
                 Separateness of External Trade from
                     the Market   94

PART III. THE SLAVE TRADE

CHAPTER SEVEN.   Whydah: Institutional Origins
                     of a Port of Trade   99
                 Ports of Trade in Early Societies   99
                 Slave Trade on the Gold Coast   102
                 Ardra: Transition   105
                 On the Slave Coast   115

CHAPTER EIGHT.   Savi: Sovereign Whydah
                     and the Treaty   126

CHAPTER NINE.   The Port of Trade Under Dahomey   131

CHAPTER TEN.   Fictitious European Money
                     in the Slave Trade   140
                 Native and European Trading   140
                 "Weight of the Measure"   146
                 Sortings   148

Contents xiii

English "Ounce Trade" and French
"Once" 154

PART IV. CONCLUSION

CHAPTER ELEVEN. Archaic Economic Institutions 173
Societal Functions
of Archaic Money 173
Cowrie and Gold 175
Cowrie from North and South 179
Cowrie Legend 184
Cowrie and the State 187
Status and State-Building 192

BIBLIOGRAPHY 195

INDEX 201

MAPS
1. The Gap of Benin 4
2. Rainfall of West Africa 7
3. Political Map: Dahomey, Oyo, and Ashanti 25
4. The Guinea Coast 103
5. The Gulf of Guinea, *circa* 1725 110
The Royal Palace
and the European Factories at Savi *endpapers*

Perspective

This book is about the economic achievements of a preliterate society, the eighteenth-century Negro kingdom of Dahomey. The focus is on the rise of Dahomey and its adjustment to that unique episode of world commerce, the modern slave trade that erupted in Dahomey's backyard. The perspective of the work as a whole is, however, anything but antiquarian. Conceived as an economic historian's modest contribution to meeting the problems of his own age, our analytical sketch is presented in the conviction that a realistic view of great socioeconomic changes, wherever and whenever enacted, broadens our horizon and advances the search for solutions. Yet even if some features of the past would seem to offer lessons for our own time, we must still beware of idealizing backward worlds.

Fear, that architect of power, is swinging in our days the axis of men's lives away from the economic order of things and toward the political and moral order. Bare physical survival, freedom, and a morally meaningful existence are the imperatives of the immediate future. Contrary to appearances, it is not material livelihood, but survival and human integrity that are the emergent issues. The magnitude of the shift sets the perspective of this book.

No lengthy regression in time is required to record the historical origin of our present entanglements. The nineteenth century gave birth to two sets of events of a very different order of magnitude: the Machine Age, a technological development of millennial range; and the market system, the initial adjustment of economic organization to that development.

Changes in economic organization were required to give

scope to the technological miracles of the nineteenth century. The market system may well have been the only means of organizing the use of elaborate expensive machinery for the purposes of production. Readiness and capacity for risk bearing, knowledge of products and of consumers were alien to the merchant class which for generations had been practicing "putting-out." In the circumstances, markets for everything had to be organized as the only effective way of assuring a steady flow of raw materials for the machines and disposal for the finished products. Failing a system of interconnected markets at all stages, the economic risk of investing capital in machinery would have been too great. Not only were markets needed for the purchase of consumers goods and raw materials, but land and labor also had to be organized as pseudo-commodities so as to assure mobility and continuity of supply. Man and his environment inevitably came to be governed by the laws applicable to the marketable commodities produced for sale. The outcome was one approaching a self-regulating system of markets, which revolutionized Western society in the first part of the nineteenth century.

The consequences for man's idea of himself and his society were fateful: Once livelihood had been organized through an interconnected set of markets, based on the profit motive and determined by competitive attitudes, man's society became an organism that was in all essential regards subservient to materially gainful purposes.

Under a market system the influence of the economy on the social process is, of course, overwhelming. The working of the economy—the interplay of supply and demand—here shapes the rest of society or rather "determines" it, almost as in a triangle, the sides "determine" the angles. Take the stratification of classes. Supply and demand in the labor market are, by definition, identical with workers and employers respectively. The classes of capitalists, landowners, tenants, brokers, merchants, and professionals were defined and actually created by the respective markets for land, money, capital, and various services. The incomes of these social classes were fixed by those markets, their rank and position by their income.

Once technology had led to a market system such an institutional setting would center man's thoughts and values on the economy. Concepts such as freedom, justice, equality, rationality, and rule of law seemed to attain their culmination in the market system. Freedom came to mean free enterprise; justice centered around the protection of private property, the upholding of contracts, and the natural verdict of prices in the market. A man's property, his revenue and income, the prices of his wares, were now just as if they were formed in a competitive market. Equality came to mean the unlimited right of all to enter into contract as partners. Rationality was epitomized by efficiency and by a maximized market behavior. The market was now *the* economic institution, its rules identical with the rule of law, which reduced all social relations to the norms of property and contract.

The modern exchange economy is a market system which includes within its scope all aspects of society that depend on material means, even though indirectly. Since very little of our social existence can be carried on without material means of one kind or another, the principles governing the economy (or the process of material supply) came to be considered as absolutes.

The new perspective calls for a different set of priorities, in which the economy must be relativized in regard to society. Our out-of-date market mentality is an impediment to a realistic approach to the problems of the era in which forgotten continents are suddenly industrializing and the industrial ones are steered by electronic automation and nuclear power toward unknown shores (Polanyi, 1947).

The largely unconscious weakness under which western civilization labors lies in the peculiar conditions under which its economic destiny was shaped (Polanyi, 1944). Having absolutized the principle of profit, man lost the capacity of subordinating it again. The very word "economy" evokes not the picture of man's material livelihood and the substantive technology that helps to secure it, but rather a set of particular motives, peculiar attitudes, and specific purposes which collectively we are accustomed to call "economic," though they are as such foreign to the actual substantive economy and came to be regarded as its corollaries only by virtue of an ephemeral interplay of modern Western culture traits. Not the permanent features of the economy but the transitory ones appeared to us as the essentials.

The obsessions of the nineteenth century may block the road to life, ideologically and institutionally. They are a paralyzing handicap in dealing with the organizing of material production under the emerging social conditions. Our perspective is then a succession of problems for life and society raised by a Machine Age of enduring character. A fairly recent innovation, the market system, inhibits the understanding of societies where no markets for labor or land existed. In the absence of these markets the working of the economy is, on the face of it, inexplicable, because there is here nothing to account for the disposal of labor and land, the factors of production. The economic historian's critical interest in archaic society naturally lies in identifying the structures, institutions, and operations by means of which the economic process is implemented.

Concepts of the economy designed to explain the functioning of a market system are certain to give biased results when applied to another institutional framework. Take, for instance, the definitions of such basic terms as trade and money. Trade is defined as a two-way movement of goods through the market as directed by prices; money, as a means of facilitating that movement; and where trade and money are given factors, markets would be postulated. Yet such an approach may be entirely misleading. In Hammurabi's Babylonia, marketplaces in the cities were altogether absent. However, this fact escaped the observation of Assyriologists. Moreover, the above concept of money is inadequate. Money is not necessarily a means of exchange. It may be a means of payment, it may be used as a standard, and different objects or material units may serve the different uses. In Babylonia, barley was used for payment, e.g., of wages and rents, while silver was used as a standard. In the absence of markets there is little evidence of exchange other than that of specific objects, such as a definite plot of land or a house, a few individual slaves, heads of cattle or a boat, and that rarely, if at all, shows any actual employment of silver. Rather oil, wine, wool, or other staples served indiscriminately as a means of exchange, at fixed equivalents.

In regard to trade the situation is similar. Trade in Babylonia, which, in contrast to Egypt, was ample, was thought by scholars to be market trade. Thus, administered trade and gift trade were overlooked; yet gift trade was the chief form of trade between the empires of antiquity. The other form of administered trade conducted from the Babylonian period onward was through that important institution of premodern times, the "port of trade."

Nor did the concept of price fare differently. Prices were taken to be obviously market prices. Actually, in antiquity prices were fixed largely by custom, statute, or proclamation, and perhaps should not generally be called prices at all. To describe them as "fixed prices" would be quite misleading, since they had never fluctuated. Possibly a new term, such as "equivalents," is needed. This is the term here employed for permanent rates at which one kind of goods either was substituted or exchanged for another. The difference is basic between these two variants of equivalents: "substituted," as in the one-way movement of payment "in kind" of taxes or as in choosing between ration goods under a point system (substitutive equivalents); "exchanged," as in the two-way movement of goods, for instance in the purchase of one sort of fungible for another at a fixed rate (exchange equivalents).

The fountainhead of all these errors was to rank exchange as *the* economic relation; hence the claim to the validity of such marketing terms as "supply" wherever things were available, or "demand" wherever things were employed as a means to a purpose. On such flimsy grounds was the human world interpreted by economists as a potential market system. Actually, patterns other than exchange obtained in the economic organization of the premodern world. In primitive communities reciprocity occurs as a vital feature of the economy; in archaic economies redistribution from a center is widespread. On a smaller scale, the pattern of the livelihood of the peasant family is householding. But reciprocity and householding, however general, remained invisible to the modern observer who would notice economic phenomena only if they were reducible to exchange.

Dahomey's economy was based on the balance of a redistributive administration and local freedom mediated through a tissue of reciprocating and householding institutions supplemented by local markets. A planned agriculture was combined with village freedom; a governmental foreign trade coexisted with local markets while avoiding a market system. This archaic society possessed a solid structure built upon the rule of law; and status was further reinforced by money functions foreign to the market system.

The economic historian should make the data of the past available in an objective light. It seems probable, for instance, that the accomplishment of literacy as a criterion of civilization should be dropped in the light of highly stratified societies that banned the art of writing for religious, political, or economic reasons, preferring isolation to undesirable culture contact. The Ashanti and the Dahomeans come to mind. How were their accomplishments in war, or in trade and currency, compatible with illiteracy? The answer lies in a forgotten phase of civilization which we might call "operational," owing to the gadgets by means of which complex mechanical and organizational feats may be performed without a conceptualization of the successful process. Some early states—prototypes of archaic society—may have emerged from primitivism precisely by virtue of operational devices, of which elaborate pebble statistics or differentiated numeration systems are a sample. There were in Dahomey, for example, the two ways of counting—the one applying to cowrie money, the other to "men and mice," i.e., all other things. These devices were an advance in communication comparable to I.B.M., which also results in replacing and surpassing thought by mechanism.

Another source of administrative achievements under the early state was a high level of statecraft. This was partly owing to the absence of a market system which later tended to replace government. Accordingly, the decay of political crafts from which the modern age suffers may have resulted from the gradual expansion of markets.

In any case, the study of eighteenth-century Dahomey reveals that the gift of statesmanship is not a European privilege. Neighboring Dahomey and Ashanti maintained an independent existence on the Guinea Coast, deliberately and skillfully using separate currencies over centuries. In spite of an extensive commercial intercourse, the rates of exchange were kept stable. Ashanti employed gold dust; Dahomey used cowrie—an elusive monetary medium as modern West African colonial powers have learned. The English and French, moreover, employed a mutually stable fictitious currency in the slave trade.

Operational civilization in native Africa is giving way to literacy; high statecraft may reappear unexpectedly in the awakening countries of that continent. Even the anxious conflicts of freedom and bureaucracy, or of planning and market, are not altogether novel. Threats to freedom from an intricate administration as well as contradictions between free exchange and central planning were foreshadowed in the archaic economies. Both these dilemmas seem to have interacted in Dahomey.

The social structure of the early state abounds in institutional devices that act as safeguards both to freedom and efficiency. The Dahomean countryside was teeming with big and small marketplaces in village and bush, yet the choice of crops was directed by planning from the capital. Overseas trade was channeled through a bureaucratic network separate from the markets, through the intermediacy of the "port of trade." Arbitrary rule was barred through the formal separation of the central administration from activities originating in familial and local life, those cradles of tradition and freedom. Such jurisdictional limitations were reinforced by the administrative divisions of defense, trade, taxation, and currency domiciled in the palace, while local autonomy was rooted in primordial custom which the king himself did not dare to offend.

Modern man, in the person of the economic historian, is for the second time penetrating into precolonial Africa. The Dahomey of eighteenth- and nineteenth-century British travelers was the home of the Amazon army, a fighting force unparalleled since Herodotus' semimythical Scythia; of pyramids of skulls, evidence of human mass sacrifice demanded by the duties of ancestor worship; and, to some extent, of religious cannibalism. This was the Dahomey from whence Bristol and Liverpool channeled war captives to the West Indies under conditions of unspeakable inhumanity. The questions raised in this book bypass as much our ancestors' unpardonable crimes against mankind as the Africans' recent acceptance of the ideals of personal freedom and progress. We must guard against being anachronistic in either direction.

Redistribution, reciprocity, and householding do not severally amount to an economic system; hence the necessarily fragmentated picture of the archaic economy. There comes to mind Karl Bücher's (1913) assertion that only modern societies possess an integrated national economy, largely based on exchange, the *Volkswirtschaft*. In the archaic economy of which Karl Rodbertus' (1865) *oikos* (as the Greeks called the "house") was the paradigm, markets were not absent, yet the economy did not possess a market system. By introducing exchange we will, however, be bringing in markets, money, and trade, the very ingredients on which Western national economies rest. This might seem to fulfill the requirements of an economic system. But though Dahomey was a country of markets, these markets, being isolated, did not link up into a system. This has been overlooked, mainly because market,

money, and trade have been erroneously thought to be inseparable. Yet contrary to eighteenth- and nineteenth-century
preconceptions, trade, money, and markets did not issue from a
common matrix, and in fact had independent origins. The
origins of trade and money are buried in the prehistory of
mankind, while markets are a more recent development.

Western thought has been almost incapable of conceiving of
trade and money except as functions of the institution of the
market. This was indeed a correct interpretation of the market
economy of modern times, where trade, money, and markets
fused as functions of the market mechanism into what strikes
us rightly as an economic system. A general integration and
recurrence of the process is produced by the forces of supply
and demand acting through markets. Over the greater part of
economic history, however, trade, money uses, and market
elements came into being and developed in relative independence from each other.

Trade is, originally, acquisition and carrying of goods over a
distance; it serves a one-sided "import interest." The element
of twosidedness entered chiefly with expeditionary and gift
trade. Money used for payment originated in definite situations, such as compensation and ritual fines. Anthropologists
and historians of antiquity have shown recently that trade and
money are frequent features of societies, but not so markets.
This is true of the market in both its current meanings: The
one is that of a *place*—typically an open space—where buyers
and sellers meet and where the necessaries of life, mainly
foodstuffs or prepared food, can be bought; the other is that of
a *supply-demand-price mechanism,* not necessarily bound to a
definite site.

The role of the exchange pattern in the Dahomean economy
reveals a number of unexpected features. While local markets,
money, and foreign trade were widely in evidence, exchange as
an integrating pattern on an economy-wide scale played
scarcely any part in the society. The reason is simple: to play a
part, exchange must function through prices that result from
market forces; under such conditions production is a function

of prices in the markets for consumers' and producers' goods.

In Dahomey none of this applied. Prices were not formed in the market but by agents or bodies external of it. Production was under the control of the monarchy, the sib, and the guild, not of an anonymous competition of individuals or firms directed toward profit made on prices. Thus exchange was barred from developing into an integrating pattern that would structure the economic process. Exchange institutions remained disconnected traits, however vital they might have been within restricted pockets of the economy.

Trade, mainly foreign trade, was institutionally distinct from markets and fell within the state sphere. Neighborhood trade, physically circumscribed by the range of the isolated market, was insignificant in volume and did not grow into middle distance trade. Even less did it merge with the redistributive flow of imports and exports handled by the central power.

The use of money, while enforced in the local markets, also fell within the control of the state which issued it and where it was vital to the functioning of the redistributive system. Money movements did not add up to "finance" as in the economies where credit played a part in the mobilization of resources. Dahomey was largely an economy "in kind" where even staple finance played a subordinate part.

In the nonstate sphere only a few of the basic requirements of livelihood were tied to the market. In the building of compound walls, the thatching of roofs, the fulfillment of obligations to parents, the cultivation and harvesting of the fields, reciprocal social institutions were at work—the *dokpwe* (labor team), the *so* (craft guild), the *gbe* (mutual aid group), and above all the *sib* (patrilineal lineage society). These allocated the uses of labor and of land, channeled the movements of the economic process, organized production and, mainly acting from outside, set prices in the market. Money and trade were in this way fitted into the redistributive sphere of the state— the taxation system was monetized, the supply of arms and other government imports depended upon a state-organized foreign trade.

While no economy-wide exchange system developed from the markets, cultural creativity found expression in each of the three exchange institutions: In regard to the market, the isolated markets are a singular development. Trade culminated in the port of trade of Whydah, an organ of commercial administration of great elaborateness and efficiency. In the field of money Dahomey produced feats of excellence, rare in the history of currencies.

The slave trade that centered on the port of Whydah stands as a challenge to the economic historian in more than one way. The word "archaic" that was dropped from systematic anthropology as merely of esthetic and cultural connotation may have to be restored to denote a sociological phase intervening between the "primitive" and the "modern." But the historian will have to apply it with caution, if he is not to find himself entangled in a circular definition. The interconnected phenomena of state and economy, institution and society—each of them sometimes called archaic—lack an authentic priority to the claim of being the name-giving category. Not states and societies, not even economies as a whole should be regarded as archaic. We shall prefer the genetic approach describing as "archaic" those *economic institutions* which do not yet appear in primitive communities but are no longer found in societies where the use of money as a means of exchange is already common.

An analysis that undertakes to present the structure and functioning of an archaic economy will meet issues that are obfuscated either by lack of empirical evidence of by the inadequacy of concepts. In this case study an effort should be made to employ clarified terms regarding the archaic economy of eighteenth-century Dahomey and its slave trade. Can we identify archaic variants of trade, money, and market institutions? Can such an economy be described as embedded in institutions patterned along the lines of redistribution, reciprocity, and exchange? What mechanisms and devices were created to permit and facilitate trade between alien cultures? And how did Western trade under the pressure of the slave rush adjust to the methods of West African commerce?

Apart from the climatic freak of the Gap of Benin and the set frame of Dahomean geography, the tragedy of the slave trade compels us to heed also the constraints of history that shaped the bed of institutional developments. We must therefore refrain from projecting our situation into the African environment, yet be ready to make use of those elements of answers to our own problems we may happen to find in this chapter of the history of mankind.

PART I

The Frame of History

CHAPTER ONE

*A*n Inland Dynasty and the Gap of Benin

When the kingdom of Dahomey appeared on the Guinea Coast in 1727, it was a new monarchy, scarcely more than a century old. It had risen suddenly from a mere aggressive local clan that had forced itself upon ethnically mixed groups in a no-man's-land to the status of a power feared for its military efficiency and admired for its elaborately organized foreign trade, its stable currency, and its exemplary administration. For the historian, such a swift ascent from an inauspicious start to the culmination of statehood presents a problem.

This Dahomey was not the Dahomey of nineteenth-century maps. It was of much smaller area and originated in the late sixteenth century on a plateau some sixty miles from the coast that was little more than a day's march across. After much fighting it expanded to the territory which eventually encompassed the people of nineteenth-century precolonial Dahomey. The vicissitudes of its history as well as the stimuli that prompted its exertions sprang from the physical mold in which it was cast, its restricted area, and its ambiguous position in relation to the coast, caused by the so-called Gap of Benin.

From the Couffo River on the west to the Weme River on the east, the country's average breadth was no more than fifty miles, an area extending to 4,000 to 5,000 square miles in all, with a population of about 200,000. It was a bare fraction of the size of the neighboring Oyo, of Yoruba origin, to the northeast. Dahomey's was a typical west African demographic

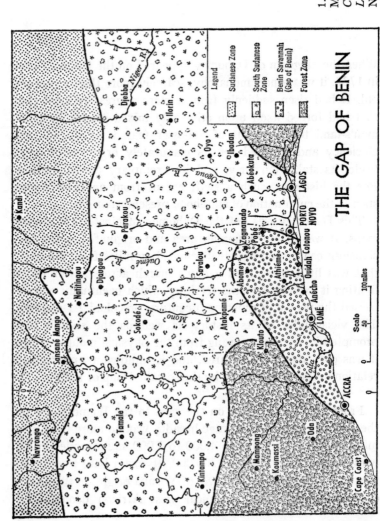

1. Slightly enlarged fragment of Map No. 2 in Paul Mercier, *Cartes Ethno-démographiques de L'Afrique Occidentale*, Feuilles No. 5, I.F.A.N. Dakar, 1954.

THE GAP OF BENIN

Legend

Sudanese Zone

South Sudanese Zone

Benin Savannah (Gap of Benin)

Forest Zone

Scale

0   50   100 miles

landscape of fragmented ethnic groups adjusted to the ecology of almost unbroken savannah, dotted with palm oil trees (*Elaeis guineensis*), and a sparse, settled population of motley peoples, obsessively fearful of the sea which was to them tabu. Dahomey's neighbors to the east and west also shunned the coast. Their capitals lay at a comparable distance to the sea as did Dahomey's own capital, Abomey; Kumasi, capital of the Ashanti; Benin City of the kingdom of Benin; and Old Oyo of the Yoruba kingdom of that name (Forde, 1960: 135).

As a geographical entity, an almost featureless area of bush country, Dahomey possessed neither natural resources nor natural frontiers, except on the river Couffo and the lake Atheme in the southwest corner. It was too small for defense in depth and lacked rivers and mountains to offer tactical advantages, though it was forested in part. Hence the dire necessity for superior arms to make up for these deficiencies. Dahomey could not altogether avoid the coast whence alone the firearms needed for survival could come. The Gap of Benin, which broke through the eastern and the western forest zones of the coast, connected inland Dahomey with the coastal lagoons. Over a stretch of less than 300 miles out of some 2,000 the coast remained unforested; and over a span of some 30 miles the rainy season became considerably milder, thereby improving the climate and, particularly on a short stretch due south of Dahomey, the fertility of the soil.

"The hole," as the French call it, represents, then, a *lusus naturae* on a grand scale. Along several thousand miles—from Senegal to the Niger—the hinterland of West Africa is approachable from the sea only at the river mouths. Paul Mercier, whose ethnodemographic charts underlie this presentation, broadly describes this West African region as follows:

It runs from the coast to the Sahara and comprises . . . the climatic and vegetational zones in their longitudinal sequence called the Sahel, the Sudan, the Baoule and the Benin. However, a fact of the first importance disrupts this order: it is the existence of the Gap of Benin by way of which Soudanese climatic influences can reach right through to the coast, thus separating the western forest region of Guinea from the central African forest region to the east. This break-through [*trouée*] takes its effect almost parallel to the Atakora mountain range which, originating in S. Togo ends in gradual decline about the W. Niger. It is neither our task, nor is it within our competence to explain this climatic anomaly. Let me refer to some remarks of J. Richard-Molard on the matter: "Starting with the Cape of Three Points (Takoradi) the coast is subject to the monsoon; a cold marine current accompanies the coast closely: the Toto-Atakora mountain chain deflects the eastern air currents flowing from the Sudan, so these can penetrate southwards; in winter, a low pressure zone over the contiguous equatorial Africa sucks in the harmattan [the dry land wind on the coast of Upper Guinea]." In brief, four plausible reasons explain why the climate is not any more that of the deep forest.

In regard to the coastal stretch that corresponds to the Gap of Benin, Mercier follows Richard-Molard's description:

Gradually the rhythm of two rainy seasons asserts itself [as one moves south-eastwards parallel to the Atakora mountain range, i.e., in the direction of the Gap of Benin]. The rainfall decreases as one approaches the coast; *Lomé,* where the mountain range starts from up the coast, registers the lowest precipitation. "The seasonal rhythm is still equatorial, but the rains are moderate; the Soudanese atmosphere does not display its crushing rigors (the local harmattan appears only as a tradewind). This is an equatorial border-range, where the palm-oil tree is already at home but cereal plants, particularly maize, still feel perfectly at ease. In short, an equatorial land, but not yet to a degree which involves the virgin forest, and thus it keeps within humanly bearable limits." (Mercier, 1954b: 4–6, and quoting Richard-Molard, 1949: 18–19, 43; author's translation.)

To this Mercier adds that this fact certainly has its human bearing and sociological importance.

Nothing was easier for the other hinterland states of Upper Guinea than to remain off the coast. But Dahomey, depending on the slave trade for the securing of firearms, had to seek direct contact with the coast, while having grave reasons to shun the resulting entanglements. That gap in the climate and vegetation thus formed an unwelcome link between the hinterland and the ocean. It shaped the history of Dahomey.

To the lagoon peoples their marginal site meant safety. Their interconnected water lanes of nearly two hundred miles were sheltered from attack in the north by swamps as at Porto

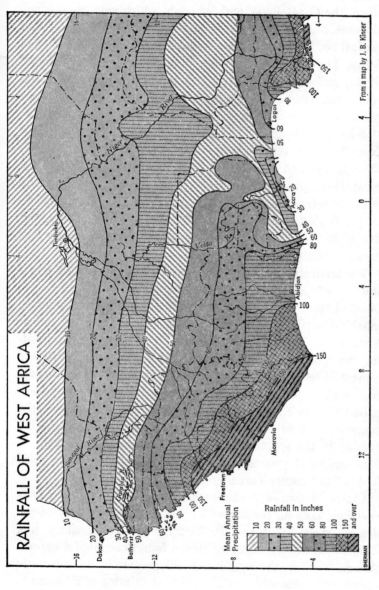

2. Fragment of *Rainfall Map of Africa* by J. B. Kincer, published with "Land Classification Map of Africa," H. L. Shantz and C. F. Marbut, American Geographical Society Research Series, No. 13, Plate II.

Novo, the Great Popo, and Whydah, which comprised island hideouts, fords, moving rivers, and narrow "passes," and other tactical bottlenecks, such as also favored the inland kingdom of Ardra. The geography of other inland states such as Ashanti, Benin, and Oyo contributed also to their security. But Dahomey was unable to remain an inland state. From the start "and for nearly a century, Dahomey could barely repel the attacks of her neighbors" (Forbes, 1851:87). The Dahomeans' dependence on the Afro-American slave trade for guns left them no alternative but to establish themselves in force on the coast. However, the network of lagoons was difficult for a land power to seize, and no less awkward to hold against the neighboring seafaring and fishing peoples sometimes openly, but mostly covertly, supported by the white navies. Dahomey was not fortunately placed in the world.

The territory of Dahomey had never formed part of a larger state-society, the fragments of which might have served as building stones of a new abode. Nor did the ethnically mixed inhabitants possess a tribal organization—such as Ashanti or Yoruba—which might have produced a federation approximating the coherence of an empire. This is not to underrate the cement of religious tradition with its cohesive power and penetrative effect on the Dahomean culture. Ancestor worship comprised also an allegiance to the royal clan which gave to the common faith of the people and their sovereign a radiating symbol in the spectacular Annual Customs with its halo of abundance and generosity. (The Annual Customs are discussed in detail in Chapter Three.)

Closer to everyday existence, rootedness in the land was sustained both on the higher level of entailed property of the descent group or sib and on the common level of village life. This was a society where existence found meaningful expression as much in the equality of villagers as in its autocratic counterpole—the monastic discipline of an army of aristocratic Amazons or the rigorous performance of his duties by the monarch himself. The French historian E. F. Gautier called the Dahomean monarchy the most advanced form of political organization in the black world (Gautier, 1935: 129–30). Admittedly, acts of repulsive cruelty, religious mass murder, and endemic techniques of treachery in the political field were the accompaniment of these high achievements. Nevertheless, Dahomey's was an unbreakable society, held together by bonds of solidarity over which only naked force eventually prevailed.

A study of the economy of historic Dahomey evokes in the modern observer admiration for the way in which the extreme of a centralized bureaucracy was made compatible with freedom and autonomy of local life. While foreign trade administration was cast in the setting of an authoritarian monarchy, the "bush," i.e., the countryside, retained a social organization that was largely outside the state sphere. The villages where the lower classes lived and the hereditary compounds which enclosed the tilled land and the entailed palm oil trees of the lineages were removed from the action of the central administration. Society as a whole consisted of a state society and a nonstate society, since the village and even more so the compounds of the sibs represented singularly state-free collectivities of households. Thus did the twin high points of Negro statecraft, the more recent monarchy and an ancient familial form of settlement, both of utmost stability and endurance, combine to produce a structure of rare perfection in its balance of spontaneity and constraint.

At the top of the pyramid the Negro state created a *sui generis* focus of power in the hieratic monarchy. It represented a near-professional type of kingship hereditary in royal families. In medieval Europe the Anjou, in modern Europe the Hohenzollern, supplied the international comity of countries with candidates to thrones. In West Africa the Ile-Ife Yoruba stocked the Upper Guinea Coast with a swarm of aspirants to the *katakle,* the squat, unadorned golden royal throne. In Ketu (some fifty miles northeast of Abomey) nine royal families (later reduced to five) accompanied the actual founding king, Ede, and ruled "in turn." From Tado, well west of Abomey, in Togo, the Adja branch of the Yoruba fanned out, starting a new holy city, Allada, from which another generation of kings spread to Porto Novo and eventually to Dahomey.

At the base of the social pyramid, where man sits on the naked soil, a form of habitation was developed which became the invariable accompaniment of Negro settlement in a considerable part of West Africa—the extended family occupying a compound made up of the houses of a man and his brothers with their wives, sons, and unmarried daughters. Several such walled groups of dwellings or compounds made up a "collectivity" (Herskovits, 1938[I]:137). In Dahomey, the compound is the residence of most male members of the agnatic descent group that Herskovits terms the "sib." An extended family, built around these men, inhabits a group of hutments or thatched houses. This pattern reflects biological, physical, and moral determinants of social behavior. Neighborhood thus serves as the foundation for the interlaced configuration of kinship, sib, and religion. An institution built in this way must attain to being as nearly indestructible as human contrivance can be.

The task of state building was arduous (*see* Chapter XI). Historical Dahomey was in the nature of a residual area left over by migrants after more coveted territories had been settled and anyhow of little use to neighbors except as an agglomeration of defenseless peoples, an easy prey to slave raids, and in the interstices of which surplus populations could be discharged if need be.

Dahomey was in fact a no-man's-land, as Paul Mercier calls it. He describes it as forming part of a power vacuum lying between the distant north and the proximate south—the north consisting of the chain of the Niger empires, Mali and Songhai, continued toward the east by the Hausa states; the south represented by the small coastal kingdoms spreading from Yoruba and Benin to Ashanti. Mercier is ready to narrow down this area further by accepting E. F. Gautier's version of a horizontal band of culture contact between east and west which cut across that vertical funnel. The eastern source of that culture zone was represented by the Yoruba, their far-reaching influence fading only in the western forest that spread inland from the Gold Coast. Mercier sees this view confirmed by the demographical evidence of slave raids resulting in a strip of low density running in that west-east band. The strip stretches through the middle Togo, Dahomey's western neighbor, to the middle Dahomey and is supposed to be in evidence even in the neighboring Yoruba region of the same latitude in the east (Mercier, 1954b:6–9).

Gautier justly claims that the equatorial forest blocs separated by the Dahomean savannah were of very different character: to the east of the Gap were the ancient Yoruban states and peoples in an afforested area with land cultivated underneath the palm trees, densely populated, and sustained by the energies that radiated from holy cities (1935:121). Over centuries a religious tradition was creating minor seats in the southwest, in Benin, and along the coast, as well as in the military center of Old Oyo in the northwest. To the west of the Gap lay the primeval forest of the Gold Coast and the Ivory Coast, down to Liberia, with high mountain ranges barring the way from a thin waste beach to an inhospitable hinterland. Dahomey itself was mostly bush. Ile-Ife and Oyo exercised their political influence from outside over a number of minor peoples of the region under their suzerainty without, however, trying to incorporate them.

The population consisted largely of fragments of migrant peoples from the east who had been moving during the course of centuries across from Yoruba to the Mono River, the western border of the Gap. Where successive waves overlapped —some had even wandered part of the way back again—their layers often were still traceable, mostly commingled with autochthonous "paleonegritic" tribes. Neither was there a political unification of the area attempted from within.

Alongside in the same general direction an elite migration also occurred which was small but vital. Sometimes followed by their friends and servants, sometimes only by their own clan, royal descendants left Ile-Ife, that cradle of kings, or the more recent holy cities to which their ancestors had moved; hence the ubiquitous monarchs with the sway of semireligious authority and truly surprising training in the performance of the royal profession. Groups of blood-relatives might alternate in offering to fill a city's throne, following one another in turn.

For the standards of the rulers of Ile-Ife vintage, we turn first to Ketu, a small, independent state close to Yoruba on the west. The most recent historian of Dahomey, a French official, was posted there the greater part of his life. The late Édouard Dunglas (1957–58), whom we here closely follow, while personally compiling the population census, reconstructed from native family reminiscences the history of Ketu since about the middle of the seventeenth century. Like Save, northeast of Abomey, Ketu was a later foundation than the much more important Yoruba offshoots of Oyo and Benin. According to oral tradition the ruler of Ketu in Dunglas' time was forty-eighth in the Ile-Ife succession, but only the last ten of these were historic. Legend kept the link with Ile-Ife unbroken by setting the date of the first migration as early as the eleventh century. Characteristic points of legend and history combined are as follows (Dunglas, 1957–58:19–21):

King Ede, who founded Ketu, was sixth in succession from the earliest royal leaders. The first of these, Itcha-Ikpatchan, left Ife-Ife for the west to seek a new home some 120 miles away for himself and his clan. Itcha camped at Oke-Oyan. As time passed, his sons separated off. One of them, Owe, trekked west; another founded Save; the third wandered farthest and became the founder of Oyo, for a long time the military capital of Yoruba. Itcha-Ikpatchan himself joined his son Owe and together they proceeded west, starting the village of Aro. When Itcha died there, Owe returned to the village of Oke-Oyan and erected a tomb to his father, staying a few years.

Altogether nine princely families of Ile-Ife had accompanied Itcha and Owe in their migration to Aro. At Owe's death his successor was selected from among the nine, and so in turn. The seventh was Ede, the historic founder of Ketu. He settled at Aro, where Itcha and Owe were eventually buried. Here the family split a second time, Ede's three sons migrating in different directions. Ede himself implored his ancestors' forgiveness, promised to have them remembered, and moved on with his faithful hunter and pathfinder, Allaloumon. The landmark sought by the guide was a huge iroko tree known to him from his rovings. Legend here merges into history.

In 1922 that tall tree was struck by lightning. It stood on the actual site of Ketu. It was here that the original settlers, of the Fon group who were to become the Dahomean aristocrats, settled in the bush and allowed migrant Yoruba space alongside themselves. Reckoning backward, according to Dunglas, 1748 is the historical date of Ede's inauguration as king of Ketu. According to tradition the ceremony occupied almost a year. Twenty-one days after the funeral of the deceased monarch, the prime minister called the Council in full session, to elect the new king unanimously from among the royal family whose turn it was. Preferably a prince would be proclaimed who had not personally always inhabited Ketu.

The person of the king elect having been thus announced to the populace, pandemonium reigned for a few hours. Rude imprecations, gross verbal insults, and maledictions against the new monarch were in order. The next morning appeasement started, all women at some time appropriated by the king were returned to their legitimate husbands, the king's private debts were arranged generously, falling back, if necessary, upon the defunct king's treasury. At a "favorable" date, set by the type of augury known as *fa,* the king's peregrinations began, preliminary to enthronement.

First the historical neighborhood sites were visited, which were linked by tradition with ancestral memories. Then the ceremonial itinerary commenced, in the course of which the monarch both symbolically and physically impersonated his predecessor Ede's traject from Aro to Ketu, from his village camp to his future capital. *En route* he had to undertake a number of intricate acts of commemoration until Ketu was reached.

The journeyings at an end, a period of ritual seclusion in three different habitations followed. During the first night of his three months' stay in the house of magic initiation, a minister of state passed on to the king the secret knowledge of soothsaying. Next morning the king left the house at dawn, with the state minister taking his place for the day. The king, entering through the High Gate, crossed the threshold of the town and stepped on to the Big Market. He was solemnly proclaimed legitimate king, his family tree from Itcha-Ikpatchan, with all its affiliations, was recounted by the herald. Another three months' stay in a particular habitation honored the memory of Ede's loyal guide Allaloumon. Eventually he spent another three months in a palace, symbolic of the city of Ife, and accordingly called by the title of the ancestral rulers, "Afin." After that the king visited a construction of straw, named after the Yoruba furnace in which iron was smelted in early times. At last the king entered the Palace. At the reception the several ministers whom he had left to take his place in the transitional habitations reappeared. The first meeting of the Council in the king's presence was held. The sovereigns of Oyo and of Ile-Ife were sent word by special messenger of the new king's accession.

So were the Ile-Ife dynasties of the eastern marshes of Dahomey installed on the *katakle* of two small kingdoms, Ketu and Save. The royal masters of the great Oyo armies that were a standing threat to Dahomey from the northeast could claim a tradition similar to King Ede's.

The Alladoxonu of Dahomey proper, to which we now turn, belonged to another branch—the western—of the Yoruba dynasty, the Adja. This sprout of the Ile-Ife had wandered in earlier centuries much farther west than Itcha-Ikpatchan and had made Tado, in North Togo, its center.

The two dynastic centers in the east, Ile-Ife and Oyo, along with another two centers in the west, Tado and Allada, were in evidence during most of the historical period. These latter were, of course, more closely affiliated to the Alladoxonu of Adja. On the plane of power, the distant Oyo was pre-eminent. Its military influence radiated right across Dahomey to its very southwestern corner, where Allada, ever in fear of Oyo, could also count on its protection if Oyo's interests happened to lie that way. Tado, capital of the northern Adja, was a geographically detached, friendly neutral, while its southern neighbor, Allada, was a problematic buffer state separating Dahomey from the coastal area and enjoying the support of the tribes of the lagoons and shallows with their fleets of pirogues.

The story of the rise of the Alladoxonu clan will take us from the western fringes of Dahomey, from which it stemmed, to the central plateau and eventually to the east until most of historic Dahomey was subjected. The earlier part of the clan's traject scarcely deserves the name of conquest, since it was more in the nature of a deft settling in the interstices, such as the Ketu dynasties practiced in the east under Ede in their quiet intrusion into the sparsely populated Fon country. Only later, when established in Abomey, does violence in a sequence of ruthless local wars play a part in the dynasty's progress toward possession of what was to become the territory of Dahomey. Regular wars against the Gede, the Ouemenou, the Tchi, and other "internal enemies" supervened.

The Adja was one of the largest of the early westward

migrating blocks of the Yoruba, and it may have been the one to move farthest from the common cradle on the right bank of the enormous delta of the Niger. Today the Adja, numbering about 150,000, occupy the former French Togo and parts of western Dahomey. The center of Adja influence was the kingdom of Tado, opposite a ford of the Mono River where the royal families that took part in the Adja migration settled. In successive accretional waves of Yoruba migrations, others followed until almost the end of the eighteenth century. The migrations were, so to speak, slow motion leapfroggings which after a pause of a generation or two propelled the next group ahead of the point that the foregoing had reached.

It was from Tado that a princely clan moved southward toward the Ardra kingdom, which also had been existing for some time off the lagoons west of the Lake Atheme. The Tado settlement of Allada on the Couffo River thus grew to be a holy city of the Ile-Ife of Tado.

Legend relates that sometime in the thirteenth century a daughter of the king of Tado had a forest encounter with a male panther, which resulted in the birth of Prince Agassou. His descendants aspired to the throne of Tado. An Adja prince was killed in the rivalry and Agassou's clan and its followers, the Agassouvi, had to leave the country. They carried with them the skull and jawbone of their deified ancestor as well as the clan's *katakle*. They settled on the Lake Atheme from whence the people of Tado eventually chased them. They chose to remove toward the northeast, where palm-oil trees grew and where they founded Allada, the eventual burial place of Agassou. Later, the Adja Tadonou began to call themselves Allada Tadonou. Historically, Allada was identical with what appears on the early maps as the state of Ardra, alongside Savi (Xavier) and Djekin (Jacquin) on the coast.

At the beginning of the seventeenth century three sons of the deceased Agassouvi king of Allada allegedly contended for the succession. The eldest, Kokpon, attained it. Te Agban-li, his younger brother, gained the throne of Porto Novo, a foundation of Yoruba tribes, while Do-Aklin, the youngest of the three, turned north and left Allada for good (Dunglas, 1957–58:83–84). His grandson was to become the first ruler of Dahomey. The last stage of his journey is a story of bravery, treachery, and murder, which makes the throne eventually acquired appear as a prize grasped by hands capable of holding on firmly.

Thus was Dahomey placed and grounded.

CHAPTER TWO

The Challenge of the Slave Trade

The historical event that subjected Dahomean society to great strain reached it from outside and happened in the economic sphere. The explosion of the slave trade which resulted from overseas plantations of sugar cane hit the Guinea Coast in the immediate vicinity of Dahomey with a unique impact.

In the last resort a geographical fact, the Gap of Benin, frustrated the inherent intent of historic Dahomey to organize as an inland state, for any sudden massive development on the coast was certain to burst the thin partition of marshy ground that separated Dahomey from the strip of small maritime states, and to make inevitable a Dahomean move to the south. The peripety brought about by the onrush of the slave trade eventually sharpened the crisis of the new state and called forth an exceptional performance on the part of the monarchy.

An epochal event as specific as the invention of the steam engine by James Watt some 130 years later had happened in the Antilles—sugar cane had been introduced into Barbados in 1640. Less than twenty years after it "had overtaken tobacco and accounted for nearly half of London's imports from the Plantations" (Davies, 1957:14–15). A dramatic transformation in Atlantic trade was set in train. Within twenty-five years the whole edifice of what came to be called the Old Colonial system was erected. The French trading company, founded in 1664, was government-financed and directed by Colbert himself.

The widely held belief that the new pattern of Afro-American commerce simply followed in the wake of the Age of Discoveries is erroneous. Actually, for another century and a half, until the rise of the sugar plantations, nothing of the sort was in sight. Only by 1683 were African Negroes—3,000 of them having been acquired in Africa for use in the colony—found in Bahia, then the capital of the overseas empire of the Portuguese. Nor were there yet significant changes in evidence on the Guinea Coast itself. Until 1664 the Guinea trade, according to Mme. Berbain, "was restricted to pepper, gold and ivory" (1942:34). In England the corresponding date was 1660, the year in which the company of "Adventurers of London trading into Africa" was founded. "Its principal objective was the search for gold" (Davies, 1957:41). Only twelve years later the Royal African Company was launched, of which its historian comments that "the new company was to deal chiefly in negroes for which there appeared to be an expanding demand in the English colonies" (*ibid.*:60). The modern slave trade can be regarded as having started in 1672.

The plantations were enormously profitable and the West Indies had become the private possession of royalty and the highest ranks of the aristocracy. The procurement of slaves was now recognized as an "absolute necessity" (*ibid.*:277). The planter's interest was given teeth through legislation. The private trader was permitted to participate in plantation profits on condition that he undertake to procure the slave labor on which that rich harvest depended. In the France of Louis XIV a government bounty was paid on every African slave exported to the Americas.

A shift in the international economy had caused a tidal wave to cross the Atlantic and to hurl itself against a twenty-mile stretch of the West African coast. This was not the usual kind of exchange of goods which by its nature enriches the people who are engaged in it. The trade that within less than a century was to sweep millions of Africans from their villages into slavery overseas was of a peculiar kind. It bore more similarity to the Black Death than to peaceful barter. The ruling strata of powerful white empires had been mesmerized by the prospect of great riches, if only they were able to provide a labor force from tropical climates for the rapidly spreading sugar plantations. The outcome was the modern slave trade.

Doubts might arise whether the new variant was really very different from the earlier; slavery being an old institution, so must the slave trade be, one might think. This would be like arguing that the Industrial Revolution of the eighteenth century could not have specific consequences, since machines had been invented and employed in production before. When all is said, the Afro-American slave trade of the eighteenth century was a unique event in social history. John Hawkins had been no more than a colorful episode. As late as 1620 an English explorer in the upper waters of the Gambia River was offered slaves by an African merchant. He replied that, "We were a people who do not deal in any such commodities, nor did we buy or sell one another, or any that had our own shapes" (Jobson, 1904:112 q. Davies, 1957:15).

The purposeful support accorded by Western governments to the slave trade was soon to produce a new configuration of commerce on the Guinea Coast. Up to the 1670's beaches from Senegambia to the Gold Coast were visited by traders; farther on they called only at Benin, the Calabars, and Angola. What was to become the Slave Coast was bypassed. Between Ardra and the Calabars no gold was found, and slaves were not yet in demand. An early English skipper's bill of lading on his return trip from Benin showed no slaves among the wares (Dunglas, 1957–58:111–12).

After 1670 the word "Guinea" in the language of trade took on an altered meaning. Formerly it stretched from the Senegal to Ardra and the Volta River—now it started there. At the same time it changed its politico-social character.

Traders had visited the northern Guinea Coast since the middle of the fifteenth century, yet no regular slave trade developed. On the off-chance of purchasing a stray fugitive from crime, a straggler or panyarred Negro shackled by an African to whom a debt was owed by the man's villagers or kinsmen, no dealings with African brokers, even less a searching of the beaches, would pay a skipper otherwise engaged in regular trade. Yet his acquisition of two or three slaves on the coast depended on just such a dribble or seepage of slaves, or tribal warfare carried on reasonably close to the shore might offer a windfall. For no African community would sell its own members into slavery except as a punishment for a very few capital crimes. Hence the beginnings of eighteenth-century slave trade tell of surprise raids perpetrated by white traders, intruding by stealth into villages off the coast. The Africans, taken in their sleep, were dragged into captivity unless they resisted, in which event they were slaughtered alongside the aged and infirm. Such a fiendish foray occurred only a few hours distant from the Ivory Coast (Smith, 1744). This was neither war nor trade. Rather, it was the sport and business of the adventuring skipper and his crew. Such manhunts could grow into a scourge to whole countrysides, either in the neighborhood of the coast or even far inland, if rivers or caravan roads offered means of transportation which stimulated the sale of captives. Unprotected bush and forest regions on which the razzias concentrated were sometimes fated to depopulation. Nevertheless, in the absence of an overseas demand requiring a regular flow of supply, the ravages of slave trading had been confined within narrow limits. Hence the organized hinterland state was fairly safe until the modern slave trade—that "enormity," to use Toynbee's term—got under way.

The beaches of Senegambia traditionally were in the hands of the Africans. No permanent relations between the foreign trader and the political sovereign were required. For orderly transactions no particular establishment on the beaches nor even treaty arrangements between the local chiefs and the white trader were needed. Gold, pepper, and ivory were regular objects of trading but no specialized slave trade developed alongside them. Even when mercantilist notions induced European governments to establish some personnel on the shore, the white man still claimed only tenant's status, not owner's. The Negro kingdoms of the hinterland jealously guarded their territory against penetration; they never ceded land. Dahomey's subsequent offer that England take over Whydah permanently was indeed a desperate step of statesmanship born of an impasse.

With the advent of sugar cane in the West Indies the rush for Negro slaves was on. Ardra was the first and most important slave trading state on the Upper Guinea Coast. Since the end of the 1660's Ardra and its tributaries, the Popos, Djekin, Lampe, Offra, Glehoue (the later Whydah), Adjache (Porto Novo) were places where inland slaves were regularly traded, most of them having passed through the territory of Ardra. By the turn of the seventeenth century the French, who had a lodge in the neighborhood, achieved permanent settlement in the coastal area of Whydah (so named after the Houeda people) and entry into the slave trade of that tribe. The Royal African Company, which previously favored the neighboring Offra, also moved its principal settlement there, "while the Portuguese became increasingly frequent visitors" (Davies, 1957:229). In 1705 the English Agent-General at Capo Corso wrote to the London office that the Whydah trade would be lost if a stop was not put to the new French settlement. Next year the English factor of the Royal African Company informed London of his intention "to enter into articles with the French," and two years later that he was renewing these articles, "the Dutch having already done so" (*ibid.*:279). (The terms of the agreement are still not known.) K. G. Davies adds that "by the early years of the eighteenth century all four of the leading slaving nations had acknowledged the advantages of Whydah as a slave-mart" (*ibid.*:229). And in a survey of prices "from the northern to the southern extremities of the company's trade," he asserts truly that they were "cheapest of all at Whydah" (*ibid.*:237).

When, in the first decade of the eighteenth century, Whydah emerged as the pre-eminent center of this new branch of world trade, the history of Dahomey took a decisive turn. The event in her close proximity was a challenge which brought the latent contradictions of her position to a head. She was now compelled to come to terms with her geographical and strategic dependence upon the coast.

The unexpected localization of the slave trade and the economic pressure of slavers' fleets off the coast undermined the inland status of Dahomey. Never before had the slave trade forced itself on an inland state of West Africa as a concern dominating its total existence. Internally and externally the supply situation was unprecedented in regard both to the numbers involved and the social wreckage caused. Not a few scores of slaves at the most were brought up annually from stray *slattees* (chained groups of slaves for sale in a market place), but many thousands of slaves were channeled in spurts of hundreds of organized *coffilas* (slave *coffles* or chain gangs). This would not have been possible without fortified lodges erected against local pillagers, even though such settlements would still be at the mercy of the concerted action of African rulers (Davies, 1957:6). Other requirements of the trade were procedures and manipulations of transporting, keeping, barracooning, subsisting, and branding adult human beings in the mass. A *modus vivendi* with the authorities of the large African states had to be found, and occasional meddling with the intricate politics of the region was inevitable (Davies, 1957:278). Benin, Oyo, and Ashanti could remain militarily aloof from the coast, with small buffer states located between them and the more densely wooded approach to the shore. The Gap of Benin, narrowing toward the south, deprived Dahomey of such a zone of insulation.

The rationale of Dahomey's policy was stringent. In her precarious military position, defense and slave trading were inseparable. Admittedly, the slave trade was also a source of very considerable revenue to the king, yet there was scarcely any room for private gain in a royal household which comprised the total expenses of army and civil service, not excluding the heavy cost of annual campaigns. Dahomey was surrounded by militarily prepared states. Acquiring slaves through intensified raiding against the weaker neighbors was impracticable. Large-scale slave wars and preventive action against over-powerful neighbors went together. Slave trading by the state, which, apart from Ardra, Dahomey alone practiced in that region, grew into a convolute of incessant wars which raised the heat of the country's devotion to the warrior's way of life beyond all normal standards. Add to this the European slavers' mercenary intent, stiffened by mercantilist bounties and bureaucratic incentives. The demand for slaves was insistent, the forts and settlements reached out for them with their ships and incited, bribed, and pressured the coastal chieftains to provide them. Dahomey, the slaver state, and the white slavers were in spite of passing differences mutual customers.

Returning to the vicious circle of Dahomean wars: three patterns of campaigns can be distinguished. Annual wars were carried on as a national institution: first, for the supply of foreign trade; to a smaller extent for the refilling of royal plantations; last, but not least, for the regular upkeep of half the male population engaged in the campaigns. Forbes called *all* soldiers traders, since the king bought from them either the head of an enemy or the live person of at least one prisoner (1851[II]:90). Every soldier to whom powder had been issued was expected to live up to this requirement or suffer punishment. To water the graves of the ancestors many hundreds of prisoners were put to death. Apart from the sacrifices at the Annual Customs, massacres of prisoners were the rule. This was a requirement of ancestor worship, the national religion. Functionally it spread fear of the king in the "bush" and helped to maintain discipline through terror.

The wars were launched under trivial pretexts or with no reasons being given. Ceremonies of mobilization heralded the event, yet the actual attack was launched in the deepest secrecy. Absence of means of rapid communication made surprise not only a part of good tactics but even of sound strategy.

A permanent constellation of power potentials underlay Dahomean wars and war threats almost all through the two and one-half centuries of the country's existence. It was fully effective in the eighteenth century, less so in the seventeenth and nineteenth. Cardinal points were: Oyo, the great power, in the northeast; a middle state, Ardra, in the south and southwest; and territorially minute Whydah, with its seaport due south. A disgruntled vassal of Oyo, Dahomey thus faced the problem of Whydah, with Oyo in the back and Oyo's ally Ardra on the flank. The power pattern did not altogether cease to operate even after Dahomey's conquest of Allada, the chief town of Ardra, in 1724. For Ardra's coastal tributaries, the Popos, and the other tribal allies remained a very real force. A campaign against Whydah had to reckon with this hostile potential, and even after Whydah was conquered the shadow of their surf pirogues haunted Dahomey's precarious tenure of the port. Moreover, the white forts and factories were always prepared to conspire with the beaten Houedas and Popos against Dahomey, the northern inland state whose supplies of slaves were exhausted time and time again owing to its excessive involvement in power politics. The Dutch, the French, and even the English commanders occasionally instigated the coastal natives to stand together to throw off the Dahomean yoke.

The national enemy was, of course, Oyo. This became an established fact in 1708, when, after a twenty-three years' effort, Dahomey succeeded in destroying the Wemenou. These were mainly a Yoruba people, densely settled along the banks of the Weme on the Dahomean side of the boundary. The disappearance of this long-stretched buffer state which separated the might of Oyo from rapidly growing Dahomey brought the power play into action. From that time onward Oyo was ever ready to crush Abomey in a preventive move. Oyo's irresistible cavalry compelled King Agadja to flee from his capital and in 1712 forced Dahomey into a condition of abject vassalage, bound to send its forces at any time against a neighbor at Oyo's bid. Dahomey was burdened with a heavy annual tribute. One item to be delivered was significant: forty-one sets of forty-one guns each (Dunglas, 1957–58:170). Oyo procured its mounts from the north but lacked firearms, which were just coming in through the southern ports.

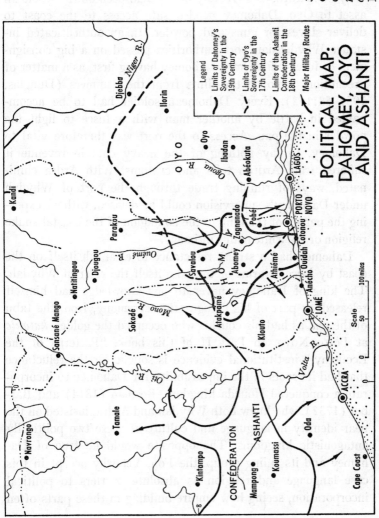

3. Slightly enlarged fragment of Map No. 3 in Paul Mercier, *Cartes Ethno-démographiques de L'Afrique Occidentale*, Feuilles No. 5, I.F.A.N. Dakar, 1954.

POLITICAL MAP: DAHOMEY, OYO AND ASHANTI

Legend

Limits of Dahomey's Sovereignty in the 19th Century

Limits of Oyo's Sovereignty in the 17th Century

Limits of the Ashanti Confederation in the 18th Century

Major Military Routes

Scale

0   50   100 miles

Dahomey possessed, to our knowledge, nothing to offer the European trader in exchange for guns except slaves, who, however, had to be captured in expensive wars on its neighbors. Only in 1818, with Oyo in decline, did King Gezo succeed in freeing Abomey from a heavy tribute and strict subservience to the formidable taskmaster. For more than a century Oyo had kept watch on the influx of arms for Dahomey by way of Whydah. Ardra, as a friendly buffer, had been on the whole an asset to Oyo. Dahomey needed safe access to the coast to deliver slaves for guns and powder. In an authenticated instance Whydensian port authorities passed on a big consignment of foreign firearms to Abomey having first, as a matter of precaution, removed the flints from the hammers (Dunglas, 1957–58:152). Every Dahomean soldier had to be accompanied in battle by another man with a fusee to light the powder in the pan. Access to the port was therefore vital to Dahomey, to say nothing of the heavy cuts in revenue it suffered from Ardran tolls and customs. With Ardra eliminated, ways of running trade through the port of Whydah under Dahomey's supervision could be devised, without exposing the person of the king to the contagion of the coastal snake religion or the white man's intimacy.

Dahomey had a strong reluctance to establish itself on the coast by force of arms or to make itself the ruler of Whydah. The king of Dahomey never to our knowledge had himself released, as part of his inauguration ceremony, from the tabu of the sea, as had his cousins who occupied the golden *katakle* at Porto Novo. In Part II of this book, "Patterns of the Economy," institutional evidence is sought for the reluctance that had its roots in the impossibility for Dahomey to incorporate a conquered Houeda kingdom. Bosman (1814) and Barbot (1732), who knew both Whydah and Ardra, insisted on the near identity in language and culture of these two politically antagonistic kingdoms. The opposite would be true of Dahomey and its ruling group, the Fon. Yet why accept in this case language and religion as absolute barriers to political incorporation, seeing how empire-building in these parts often proceeded irrespective of such obstacles? Those patterns reflected the internalization of a way of life which forbade amalgamation.

The attack proceeded by stages. The seizure of Ardra in 1724 (Smith, 1744:169) was followed by a move against Savi, the political capital of the Houeda kingdom. The conquest of Whydah, the economic capital, followed only after the European factors were advised and requested to stay neutral. But abandonment of the enterprise, or even a temporary retreat, would have meant giving up hope of emancipation from the humiliating subservience to Oyo. Even the European traders were hard put to brook the indignities to which the sudden wealth of the coastal buffer states exposed them. The Royal African Company's agent was retained in Porto Novo two years and was made to do slave labor under pretense that his company owed the king a debt (Snelgrave, 1734:66–8). Porto Novo, together with Ardra and Whydah, enjoyed the privileges of compulsory intermediaries between the white traders and Dahomey. Customs were inordinately raised by Porto Novo as well as by Whydah, which also claimed the right to "first refusal" from imports and over and above arbitrarily cut off Dahomey from European prestige goods.

Symbolic of the broad logic of challenge and response were the distressing circumstances that gave rise to some of Dahomey's great achievements. The conquest of Whydah in February, 1727, was far from final. The Houedan King Huffon had fled with a part of his army into the marshes of Atheme and Great Popo, where the landbound Dahomeans were unable to follow them. His caboceer, Assu, courageously fought his way back to Whydah, setting up camp between the French and the English settlements, Saint-Louis and Fort William's, but was chased away by a Dahomean counterattack (*ibid.*:116). The Houeda succeeded in letting Oyo have word of their plight. Oyo cavalry descended upon Abomey, sending King Agadja into the bush for refuge. Trade was hard hit, enough to make the European factors regret the change. The English governor, the unfortunate Testefole, persuaded the Houedas to join with the Popos and recapture Whydah. The Dahomeans had with-drawn their garrison from Savi and were amazed to learn that a convoy of slaves sent to Whydah found the port in the hands of a Houedan army 15,000 strong, which they believed dispersed in the marshes.

In this extremity Agadja decided to arm a company of female elephant hunters he had inherited from his father. They had hitherto served only as a bodyguard, but were now to form a regiment to make up the rear and—at least visually—swell the ranks. The daring experiment culminated in the justly famed institution of the "Amazons." This large elite force of a volunteer army of virgins was domiciled around the court, and its veterans were pensionable. This inventiveness of the Alla-doxonu dynasty was an asset to the new state in its struggle for survival under arduous circumstances, but the secret source of success was the moral cohesion uniting the state and nonstate factors in Dahomean society.

If, in a general way, Dahomey's history might be regarded as a manifold response to the challenge of the Gap of Benin, this is undoubtedly true of the economy of Dahomean Why-dah. A noncommercial inland nation was to adapt this port to a trading task of extraordinary magnitude and complexity. There is no need to enlarge on the technicalities of transacting the intricate business of the slave trade with many European countries and with brokers from numerous inland peoples. The entrance of foreign goods had to be technically and financially administered; weights and measures concerted; cultural con-tacts controlled while insulating internal trade from all avenues of unwanted external influences, particularly those which ac-company the penetrative effects of foreign currencies. We will see how the port of trade organization admirably answered these apparently conflicting requirements.

Consider the currency situation. Whydah was a small king-dom with the two hinterland regions of Dahomey and, some-what further to the northwest, Ashanti for neighbors. The statesmanship of Dahomey and Ashanti was, we should as-sume, aware of the importance of maintaining separate and distinct systems of currencies for the sake of the political and cultural integrity of their countries. Coastal Whydah, even after its political subjection by Dahomey, which always kept it culturally at arm's length, remained a *corpus separatum*. European company officials and African traders of various extraction intermingled freely. Many of the latter were of Afro-American background, Portuguese mulattoes, and repatriated African slaves. This was a place of multiple currencies, while Dahomey and Ashanti had succeeded in keeping their monetary systems separate in the face of what must appear to the modern mind as almost insuperable obstacles. Dahomey used cowrie exclusively, in elaborate, never-changing division, maintained at an unvarying exchange rate of 32,000 cowries to one ounce of gold—an amazing feat. Ashanti used gold dust as a currency, nuggets being appropriated by the king; cowries were banned in Ashanti as was gold dust in Dahomey. In Whydah under Dahomean rule both were current. Silver, the domestic currency of the various European nations, was of small account in Whydah since no coins were current, but it was commonly melted down to serve for ornaments.

Again, in foreign relations the onrush of the slave trade called forth an unprecedented expedient on the part of the Alladoxonu. West African hinterland states never relinquished any of their territory to the European powers. This was more than keeping jealous guard over sovereign rights. Dahomean religion dedicated the soil of the country to the gods and denied to the king the right of alienating any part of it. This policy was reversed by the Alladoxonu rulers and the reversal was steadfastly adhered to. The traditional attitude would have committed Dahomey to hold on to the possession of Whydah at all cost and, as a consequence, doomed the country to vassalage to Oyo, while all that Dahomey needed was the assurance of a free import of arms. Her solution was to seek close cooperation with the great power that owned the strongest fleet.

There is documentary evidence of Agadja's endeavors to cooperate with the English, even prior to his attack on Whydah. His contacts dating from Bulfinch Lambe, the first white man to visit Abomey, can be reconstructed from documents (cf. Bulfinch Lambe's letter in Smith, 1744:171–89). Captain William Snelgrave arrived in desolated Whydah only a few weeks after it was sacked and was promptly met in neighboring Djekin by Agadja's messenger with the king's invitation to proceed to Allada for consultation. Eventually Dahomean policy matured to the grand decision of offering to cede the sovereignty over Whydah to the English on sole condition of a guaranteed supply of arms to Dahomey. Bulfinch Lambe, after a two years' enforced visit at Agadja's court, was allowed to leave, laden with presents, having promised to return with a whole colony of Englishmen. Unavailing efforts to persuade the London government to accept Whydah continued under successive rulers (cf. Commodore Wilmot in Burton, 1893 [II] :252). Indeed, this perseverance appeared not unreasonable under the circumstances, but the Colonial Office refused even to consider the king of Dahomey's offer.

By the first half of the nineteenth century Oyo was in decline. Fulbe cavalry had pushed back the frontiers of the Yoruba kingdoms, and the seceding Egba had set up the fortress of Abeokouta. King Gezo of Dahomey freed his country from the shameful burden of the tribute and the military overlordship of the Oyo. Dahomey could now feel secure within its frontiers, and with the falling off of the slave trade could shift her economy to the export of palm oil. Eventually Abomey fell to French artillery, though defended by an Amazon army still possessed of all the soldierly virtues. Superior technology was victorious over a nation of great gifts exercised on an exceptional institutional level.

PART II

Patterns of the Economy

Paul Mercier describes Dahomey as a highly centralized kingdom where the local life of religion and village was nevertheless intense. In the economic field we can also distinguish a centralized domain of the state proper, and alongside it a fairly state-free body of society. The state sphere of the economy is presented in Chapter Three; the state-free field of the economy in Chapters Four to Six. In the state sphere redistribution was the main pattern. That is, the movement of the goods, whether actual or merely dispositional, was toward a center and out of it again. In the nonstate sphere, that is, the familial and local orbit, reciprocity and householding were the dominant patterns. In the absence of a market system exchange was only secondary since it did not comprise labor and land, and even commodity markets were isolated and did not form into a system.

CHAPTER THREE

Redistribution: The State Sphere

The monarchy was the central institution of the state sphere. It was accepted as of divine origin. The king was the link between the people and the deified ancestors, as well as the guardian of the people's livelihood. As such, the king played a central role in the Dahomean economy. It was he who annually reviewed economic conditions, formulated plans for the future, distributed a minimum of cowrie to the population to buy food, set certain equivalents, received and dispensed gifts, and levied tolls, taxes, and tribute.

ANNUAL CUSTOMS

The place of the monarch in Dahomean life came into focus at the great redistributive ceremony of the Annual Customs. On this occasion the king appeared before an assembly of all Dahomey to discharge his various duties as sovereign. The Annual Customs was the principal event of the economic cycle. In terms of gross national product and foreign import, as well as popular participation, it was an economic institution of unique proportions. The king himself was the central actor in an assembly of all the personages, administrators, and office holders of the land, in which literally every family was represented by at least one member for part of the time. In a day-long performance the king received gifts, payments, and tributes, subsequently distributing a part of this wealth as gifts to the crowd.

The economic aspect of the process may be analyzed as a

move of goods and money toward the center and out of it
again, that is, redistribution. It was the main occasion of
building up the finances of the royal administration and of
distributing cowrie and other imports among the people. It
took care of the remuneration of all higher officials to whom
valuable rewards of brandy, tobacco, silks, robes, carpets, and
other luxuries were dispensed. Foreign traders and business-
men contributed considerable sums to the king's revenue while
native administrators, occupying lucrative posts, handed a
share of their revenue to the king. These payments were not
always made publicly, while the royal return gifts were staged
with a view to the utmost effect.

Held each year upon the return of the Dahomean army from
the wars, the Customs was symbolic of the religious and political unifications of the peoples of Dahomey under the Alladoxonu kings. It was the occasion upon which the people did honor
to their ancestors and gave thanks for victory in battle. The
king was the mediator between the living and the dead. He
sacrificed large numbers of captives, "watering the graves" of
his forebears with the blood of the victims and recommitting
the nation to the care of the ancestral spirits. These observances were repeated on an even vaster scale at the Grand Customs, which marked the period of public mourning following
the death of a king of Dahomey and the accession of his successor.

The Customs expressed the core values of Dahomean life.
Herskovits writes:

In the life of every Dahomean, his ancestors stand between him and the
gods . . . the respect and worship of the ancestors may then be thought
of as one of the great unifying forces that, for the Dahomean, give meaning and logic to life. (1938[I]:238)

William Snelgrave, with the point of view natural to a
trader, asked a high Dahomean military official why the Dahomeans should sacrifice so many captives when these could be
sold to good advantage. To which the officer replied:

It had ever been the custom of their Nation, after any Conquest, to offer
to their God a certain number of Captives. (1734:46–47)

Burton says:

Human sacrifice in Dahomey is founded on a purely religious basis. It is a touching instance of the King's filial piety, deplorably mistaken, but perfectly sincere. The Dahomean sovereign must . . . enter Deadland with royal state, accompanied by a ghostly court. . . . This is the object of what we have called the "Grand Customs."

And, Burton continues, after every military campaign,

decorum exacts that the first fruits of war and that all criminals should be sent as recruits to swell the King's retinue. (1893[II]:13,14)

Every event in which the king was involved, whether being visited by a white man or merely moving to another palace, had to be reported to the ancestors by some male or female messenger. No prospect of additional profit through the sale of slaves would induce the king to spare a single victim from the number required.

The Customs was the occasion for a collection and redistribution of goods on a grand scale. All Dahomeans of any note, including all who held office, attended the ceremonies in person, bringing gifts to the king. The Europeans in Whydah, as well as emissaries from African sovereigns, were expected to present themselves before him, likewise bearing gifts. During the festivities, which continued for weeks at Abomey, the king himself made disbursements to the population. As many as thirty or forty thousand people might be present. On the platform erected for the king and members of his court, cowries, rum, cloth, and other fine goods were heaped up to be scattered among the crowds by the king or the dignitaries of the court day after day as the ceremonies continued (Dalzel, 1793:xxiii ff., 121 ff., 146–47). A great variety of goods was distributed items coming from as far away as Europe and India, in addition to manufactures such as fine cotton cloth from neighboring countries. The size of the contributions to the king varied greatly. Lavish gifts were expected and received from the traders on the coast (Forbes, 1851[II]:173). One of them later complained that he had brought with him the value of his year's profits as gifts for the king.

The captives taken in battle were presented to the king at this time and the king in turn accorded public recognition to his warriors and officials by making gifts of slaves to those who distinguished themselves. These formal gift exchanges celebrated Dahomey's wealth and power, and reaffirmed the mutual relations and obligations between king and people.

ARMY

Men and materials of war were collected and distributed by the monarch. Each year after the harvest, the king went to war leading an army, estimated at up to fifty thousand, including followers, into the field. This was no less than about one-fourth of the total population. The standing army was, as we saw, composed entirely of women of remarkable physique and fierceness in combat. This contingent was supplemented by annual provincial levies on the male population. A minimum of military training was assured to all young males by assigning to each soldier in the field a young boy as attendant "to be trained up in Hardships from their Youth" (Snelgrave, 1734:79, q. Herskovits, 1938[II]:80).

The organization of the army was decentralized. While the general command was exercised by the king's officials, the caboceers or top officials of the various towns and regions led their own forces into the field. The caboceers were expected to place their men at the army's disposal for the campaign and some of them, such as the king's traders at Whydah, owned thousands of slaves and supplied whole regiments for the annual slave hunt. The rank of Ahwangan, or war captain, according to Burton, "includes all officers that can bring ten to a hundred dependents or slaves into the field" (1893[I]:147, n.3).

While the soldiers were provisioned by their own masters, certain foodstuffs, such as honey, were collected and stored by royal officials for the use of all the troops. The caboceers were entitled to the booty taken by their own soldiers: "The caboceers, whose soldiers captured them, were always considered to be the owners of the slaves taken in the war," the king told

Duncan (1847[II]:264). The Amazons constituted the private army of the king and their booty belonged to him.

The separation of the civil power and the military power provides another example of the institutional divisions in which Dahomey abounded. The army was under civilian command except on the field of battle. The Mingan and the Meu, who commanded the right wing and the left wing respectively, were the highest ranking civil officers of the kingdom. Under the Mingan was the Gau, the military commander-in-chief, and corresponding to him on the left wing was the Po-su. The Gau assumed command of the armies in the field, taking precedence even over the king. In civilian life, the king always occupied the highest stool, but on the battlefront the king sat on a low stool, while the Gau sat on a higher one.

A meticulous disposition was made of captives taken in battle. After reserving a sufficient contingent for the sacrifices to the ancestors, there were set apart a number of captives corresponding exactly to the Dahomeans lost on the field of battle. These were eventually distributed to the royal plantations to replace the losses. The balance of the captives was divided into three parts: one part going to the king for his household; a second to be sold by the king as slaves; and the third to be distributed among the warriors and chiefs as a reward for valor.

Once assigned to the royal plantations, slaves could not be diverted for resale. Snelgrave complained of his unsuccessful attempt to buy additional slaves from the king:

I understood afterwards the King had no Slaves by him for sale, tho he had great Numbers of captive Negroes, which tilled his Grounds, and did other work. For it seems, after they are once enrolled for that Service, his Majesty never sells them unless they are guilty of very great Crimes. (Snelgrave, 1734:106–07, q. Herskovits, 1938 [II]:97)

ECONOMIC ADMINISTRATION

While devastating famines are not infrequent occurrences in the Niger region to the north, there is scarcely any record of famine throughout Dahomey's history. We may judge the

success of the Dahomean agricultural policy thereby. This fact
is especially remarkable because of the toll in manpower and
resources exacted by an annual war, and because the bush
stood as a constant threat to the cultivators, encroaching upon
the cultivated land as soon as effort was relaxed.

"The King of Dahomey enforces cultivation over all his
dominions," Duncan writes (1847[II]:310). And the king
himself tells Duncan "that he had long ago issued orders that
all the spare land in and around the town [of Whydah] should
be cultivated with a view of lessening the chance of epidemic
diseases" (*ibid.*:268–69).

In the injunctions to a new village official, delivered upon the
occasion of his ceremonial installation before the king and his
court, the king's policy in regard to the rural economy is
clearly stated:

The King has said that in Dahomey a chief must see to it that everyone
holds firmly where his hand rests. . . .

. . .

The King has said that Dahomey is a vast land, and that everyone must
confine his work to the place where he lives. That is why it is forbidden
to any of the young men who cultivate the earth to stop work in the fields
while the grass remains uncut.

. . .

The King has said that a country must be loved by its . . . [people] and
that is why he has forbidden his people to migrate from one part of the
country to another, since a wanderer can never have a deep love for his
land. (Herskovits, 1938:67)

. . .

The permanent administration of agricultural affairs was in
the hands of the "Minister of Agriculture," the Tokpo; under
him were the Xeni, the chief of the "great farmers" or *gletanu*,
and his assistant.* Every important official was a plantation
owner and thus a member of the *gletanu*. It was the duty of the
agricultural officials to insure a balanced production of crops
and adjust resources to requirements. Principal crops were
grown in different areas of the kingdom. For example, in a

* The main source for the material on the administration of agriculture is
Herskovits, 1938[I]:112–25.

district not far from Abomey only millet was grown; in other areas only yams or maize. In the area between Whydah and Allada, maize and manioc were the chief crops. If there was overproduction or underproduction of any crop, the farmers were ordered to shift from one crop to another. As Paul Mercier says, "In economic matters there was a strict control, not only of exported products—palm oil—but also of food crops" (1954c:210). If supplies of grain were short, no export of grain was permitted. Pigs, the chief source of meat, were counted and orders might be given banning slaughter or sales for a certain period in order to replenish stocks.

From early times on, conservation measures were undertaken by the king. The output of palm oil was safeguarded by the king's ruling that no palm wine could be made except from the palm trees growing wild in the bush, since the making of palm wine destroyed the young trees under cultivation (Burton, 1893[I]:84, n.1). During the growing season for crops, the king decreed that all animals should be tied up to keep them from trampling the new crops.

Other products were likewise subject to administrative controls. At Whydah two quarters in the town were set aside for salt-workers and the output of these workers was supervised by the viceroy of Whydah and the "salt-officials" of the court. Tradition held that the king wished no revenue from salt since it was a necessity of life, hence the tax-in-kind on salt was smaller than that on other products. Moreover, salt had to be sold to anyone who needed it, *even if he could buy only one cowrie's worth.*

The total output of honey was reserved for the use of the army and no private production or sale was permitted. Ginger was regarded as a medicinal product; as with honey, private production or sale was prohibited and distribution was handled by royal officials for medicinal purposes only. Private persons were permitted to grow pepper on a quota basis, each owner of a field being allowed the number of pepper plants that would yield one raffia sack of pepper for his own use. Certain districts were set aside for the production of pepper for the market, and a tax in cowries was levied on pepper in transit from these districts. Ground nuts could be grown only in quantities sufficient for private use. According to Burton, the cultivation of coffee, sugar cane, rice, and tobacco was banned in the neighborhood of Whydah; for what reason we do not know, but probably because these were regarded as undesirable luxuries.

The king's responsibility for the food supply of the kingdom was manifested in the relation of the crown to local markets. The marketplace had to be consecrated by human sacrifice, and since none but the king could take human life, the market had to be directly instituted by the crown. All markets were established by authorization of the king, and officials stood in attendance in the marketplace to insure order and obedience to the regulations. As noted, no food could be purchased in the market except with cowrie. The distribution of cowries from the royal hand during the Annual Customs was the means of providing the general population with the currency to buy food. Similarly, all visitors to the court were given gifts of cowries by the king, should they wish to buy food in the market over and above that provided by the king's hospitality, and, in token of permission to depart, visitors were "passed" with cowries, as the saying went, to enable them to buy food on the return journey.

CENSUS

The redistributive system of the palace economy was linked with an extensive apparatus of planning and administration.* Many of the economic affairs which made their appearance on the agenda of the Annual Customs were the concern of the royal administration throughout the year. The livelihood of the people was a charge upon the monarch. Indeed, his responsibility extended to every phase of the economy, so that much administration was carried out in the course of preparation for the ensuing Customs.

* The main source for this section and the following section on taxation is Herskovits, 1938[I]:107–34; [II]:72–79. References to the census also occur in Le Herissé, 1911:84.

Immediately after the close of the great rainy season, when the harvests had been completed, the king began preparations for the annual military campaign. This marked the time for undertaking the census which provided the data for making levies and collecting taxes. The census covered population, agricultural and craft production, livestock, and most other products and resources of the kingdom.

Care was given to the manpower resources. A total count was taken of the population and of the numbers of workers in each occupational category: cultivators, weavers, potters, hunters, salt-workers, porters who carried goods, blacksmiths, and also slaves. Following the enumeration of the cultivators, a count was made of the agricultural produce stored in granaries, of palm trees throughout the kingdom, of the number of cattle, sheep and poultry, and the output of the various crafts. After these data were gathered, taxes were assessed on the whole produce of the kingdom: grain, palm oil, salt, craft products, etc., from which provisions were secured for the forthcoming campaign. Each chief's report to the king of the population figures for his village formed the basis for the assignment of men to the different divisions of the army. Employed in the census were ingenious administrative devices which served operationally as substitutes for written records. But the main reason why the countrywide census involved so little bureaucratic harrassment was the participation of the population which willingly obeyed the law and responded spontaneously to the rules. The census data then provided the basis for the levies in kind and cowrie, which were the substance of the flow of goods and services to the state under a redistributive pattern.

The data on population gathered during the census were a state secret, known only to the king, and any village or provincial chief who disclosed the figures for his group would have been garrotted.

The census of population (cf. Herskovits, 1938[II]:72 ff., whom we follow closely) was carried out as follows: In the palace, under the charge of a woman official, were thirteen boxes, each divided into two parts, one part for males, one part for females. As each birth was reported to the king by the village or district chief, a pebble was placed in the proper section, according to the sex of the infant. At the end of each year, all the pebbles were moved up one box, leaving the first box empty, in which to begin again the recording of births during the coming year. The pebbles in the thirteenth box were thrown out, since children who had reached the age of fourteen were considered adults and were enumerated in the annual count of adults. In another room of the palace, the boxes recording deaths were kept and the count made in a similar manner. Reports of deaths in each district were relayed to the palace and two army chiefs were charged with the task of reporting the number of men killed in battle. The counting of slaves and captives was entrusted to two other officials. With their reports made, the total tally could be arrived at.

Sacks containing the census tallies for each village were placed in four large bags: one each for men, women, boys, and girls, and each sewn with the corresponding symbol—short trunks for men, beads for women, the male sex organ for boys, and a small figure with the female sex organ for girls. In addition, there were three other sacks: one in black representing men killed in battle, one in red representing deaths from illness, and one in white indicating captives.

In taking the count of adult Dahomeans, males were enumerated first. Some ten to twelve days before mobilization, the head of each family group was required to report the number of males over thirteen years of age in his group. The village chief kept a record of the count by placing pebbles in a sack for each male reported to him. On the sack was sewn a symbol indicating the village from which it came. A basketmaking village, for instance, might have a basket for its emblem. These sacks were brought to Abomey by the village chiefs themselves or by the district chiefs to whom the sacks were turned over by the chiefs of each village. As each chief presented himself before the king, he was told the army corps to which men from his village were to be assigned.

After the army had been assembled, the count of females took place. The commander of each army unit was instructed to ask each of his soldiers the number of women in his family. These were likewise recorded in pebbles, village by village, and sent to the palace. The women belonging to families whose men had not gone to war that year were counted later when a commission of war chiefs received a report from each village on the number of men who had not appeared for the campaign. It was at this time also that a check was made on how well the villages had complied with the call to arms. No military quota was assigned to each village. After the war was over, however, and the army commanders had reported how many men from each village answered the call, this number was checked against the pebbles recording the total male population of each village. Should the soldiers number less than half the total male population of the village, the village chief was strangled.

The procedure for the economic census and taxation of livestock (cf. Herskovits, 1938[I]:116 ff.) was as follows: The king initiated the annual census of pigs by calling the three hereditary chiefs of the butchers to report the names of the villages in which they bought their pigs. Thereupon a message was sent to the village named, summoning the chiefs and all those who had pigs for sale, on the grounds that the king was about to set a new price for pigs. A count of the number of pigs in each village was taken by the chief of the village before his appearance at court, and this provided a check on the accuracy of the reports made by each villager as to his stock of pigs. A complicated system of controls was then set in motion. First an order was given to the villagers, banning any slaughter of sows for the next six months. This was intended to keep the number of sows at the current level so that this figure could be taken as a constant in subsequent calculations of the total. Secondly, an order was issued to all toll posts throughout the kingdom to prevent any pigs from being carried through the gates. And finally, every market official was ordered to bring to the palace the heads of all pigs sold in the market during the next six months. At the end of this six-month period, village chiefs reported the number of male pigs in their villages, and this count, plus the number of heads delivered at the palace during the period, was supposed to be at least as large as the total reported at the beginning of the period. If it were found that too many pigs had been slaughtered and sold, the sale of pork was ordered suspended for a year. The animal tax was based on the data thus collected. Slaughterers were taxed according to the number they had handled, and in addition, everyone who raised pigs was assessed a basic toll of one animal per year.

For other livestock—cattle, sheep, and goats—control was less systematic. A census of these animals was taken only about every three years. On such occasions an impending "catastrophe" would be announced by a crier in the market place, perhaps an epidemic among the cattle, a drought, or other calamity invented for the occasion. All owners of cattle would be instructed to bring a cowrie shell for each animal as an offering to placate the gods, and these shells were collected from all over the kingdom. A female official in the palace set aside a pebble for each cowrie, keeping the piles separate for each type of animal, and placed each set of pebbles into a separate sack before sending the cowries to the temple. A symbol sewn on each sack indicated the type of animal enumerated therein—a horn for cattle, a beard for goats, weeds and a tongue for sheep; and if pigs were included in this census, a butcher's knife on the sack for pigs. The tax was based on this count, each village giving a certain percentage of its stock to the palace, about twelve and one-half per cent in the case of goats. The count was made by taking five animals out of every forty, or every eighth animal.

TAXATION

Sources of royal revenue other than the palace and its plantations were a comprehensive system of taxation, levies, and contributions. Taxation in Dahomey was general and was linked to an efficient system of collecting, accounting, and control. Indirect techniques were often used for double-checking on evasion of taxes (cf. Herskovits, 1938[I]:107 ff.). All the produce of the kingdom was taxed as well as internal trade, and the tax system was linked to various measures of economic planning and control discussed in the following section (cf. also Le Herissé, 1911:82–91 and Foà, 1895:274 ff.).

Meat was supplied to the palace by various groups of hunters. Hunting was an important source of meat for the population as a whole. Consumption of the meat of wild animals probably exceeded that of domestic ones and the annual hunt is still a feature of Dahomean life. There were two hunting chiefs at court, one for hunters and one for fishermen, and a hunting chief (*dega*) in each village. A count of the hunters was taken annually in the course of ceremonial observances at the shrine of the deity of the hunt near Abomey. On the basis of this count, the *dega* were divided into thirteen groups, four *dega* for each Dahomean month, and each of the thirteen groups was required to furnish meat for the palace during one month. In addition, the heads of all animals killed were sent to the palace to decorate the entrance. A tax on fishermen was paid in dried fish, and presumably collected by means of procedures similar to those for hunters.

With regard to domestic animals, as we have seen, all who kept pigs were assessed one animal per year. Slaughterers were taxed on the basis of the number of animals they had killed. Cattle, sheep, and goats were taxed every three years, a certain proportion of the animals being taken, such as 1 in 8 for goats. Horses belonged only to certain individuals of high status. A tax of 4,000 cowries a year was collected for each horse.

Contributions of honey, pepper, and ginger were made by two districts near Abomey devoted to the cultivation of these products. These products were regarded as military stores and their production was closely supervised.

The taxation of salt was also based on a close supervision of production. Salt was obtained by the evaporation of sea water, and production was limited to the coastal town of Whydah. The salt-workers, resident in two quarters of Whydah, were required to dig hardpans where the process of evaporation was carried out, and permission for digging had to be obtained from the king's deputy. From each salt-worker the king required ten sacks of salt—about eight kilograms—each year. These sacks were deposited with the viceroy of Whydah, who set aside a pebble for each sack received, sending these "salt pebbles" to Abomey at stated times. At Abomey the pebbles were counted in sets of ten to determine the number of salt-workers represented. A separate check on the honesty of the viceroy was made by sending another official from the court to the salt-workers' quarters at Whydah to count the number of salt pans set out. This count had to tally with that submitted by the viceroy, and any discrepancy was a grave offense for which the viceroy might be punished by being deprived of his revenues of office for the period of a year. From the proceeds of this tax the king supplied his household, perhaps also the army.

The forge was the unit for accounting, taxation, and other administrative measures relating to iron. Twelve forges throughout the country were designated to make hoes; and production of hoes was limited to these forges, each of which was under the watchful eye of an official charged with supervising production. Since no hoes could be sold directly from the forge, all sales had to take place in the market under the supervision of market officials. The market head or his deputy had to witness every sale of hoes, recording the sale by placing a pebble in a box marked with the device of the forge at which the hoe was made. Every forge had its device. It was stamped on the product of the forge, and copies of all the devices were registered with the palace and distributed to all market officials. There were twelve boxes in the keeping of each market head, one for each forge, and as each box was filled it was sent to Abomey and replaced from the capital. A supplementary count of production was taken by summoning smiths to the palace to determine how many hoes were made at their respective forges. From the total thus reported, the number of hoes sold in the market was deducted, leaving the total number on hand. The tax was based on this count, each ironworker being given a token bar of iron by the king and instructed to return with a specified number of cartridges, more or less in number according to the quantity of unsold hoes remaining at the forge.

Other smithies not engaged in making hoes were enumerated through the priests who served the god of iron (*Gu*). Each forge had its shrine to the deity, and at specified times the priests were called together to receive from the hand of the king the cocks needed for the annual ceremony to the god. The number of forges in the kingdom was then calculated by deducting the number of cocks given out to the priests from the total number on hand at the palace before the distribution to the priests. In addition, the number of smiths was determined by asking each priest how many men worked at his forge.

The weavers and wood cutters likewise were assessed a certain proportion of their product.

Internal trade also was taxed. A "passport" system was used in keeping count of porters who carried goods through tollhouses and in levying the taxes on such trade. There was a tollhouse at the entrance to every town, at certain places on the lagoons, and at the doors of European trade establishments. During the Annual Customs,

the public crier was sent to the markets to announce that all porters must declare themselves before a given official. . . . As the men reported, each gave his name and, in secret, proffered some kind of sign to constitute his passport. Thus, one might employ a small chain, counting the links, so that there would be one for each tollgate through which he must pass, the other links of the chain being distributed among the keepers of the gates. Another might give a small raffia-cloth . . . replicas of these cloths being also distributed to all officers at the toll-posts. When . . . this porter . . . arrived at a toll-post, he was asked for his "passport" and produced the cloth. This was then compared with the cloth that had already been received by the keeper and if there was even a minor difference between the two, the carrier was bound and sent to prison. (Herskovits, 1938[I]: 130–31)

The method of levying the tax was as follows:

A small pebble was set aside at each toll-gate every time a given porter passed through it, and at the end of the year the amount he was assessed was based on the number of trips he had made. (*Ibid.*:131)

Other taxes were facilitated by the enforcement of carrying. For example, pepper, except for limited quantities, could be produced only in certain districts which were located at some distance from the market. This enabled a tax in cowrie shells to be levied on the goods in transit.

Taxes-in-kind in local markets were taken in the form of "samples" of each type of produce sold in the market (*ibid.*: 127–28). Forbes remarks, however, that "collectors stationed at all markets . . . receive cowries in number according to the value of the goods carried for sale" (1851[I]:35).

A poll tax on every inhabitant of Dahomey is mentioned by Duncan. For certain individuals this might be very high. For example, two slaves of the Viceroy of Whydah are reported to have paid an annual head tax of $1,500 and $2,500 in cowries (Duncan, 1847[I]:122–23).

The death of an official was accompanied by an inheritance tax levied as follows: first, the possessions of the deceased were brought to the king's palace at Abomey. Then the king decided whether the deceased's son was to assume his father's official position or whether it would be awarded as an honor to someone else, such as a soldier who had distinguished himself in battle. Only if the son was reappointed would he inherit his father's wealth. Since the king had overall title to property and land in Dahomey, the return of his father's property had the status of a gift. At the same time, a portion of the inheritance was retained by the king (Herskovits, 1938[II]:6).

The basic tax was that on all agricultural produce. Each year after the harvest, the "minister of agriculture," the *Tokpo,* and his assistants counted the granaries in the kingdom where the crop was stored, recording separately the supplies of maize, millet, peanuts, beans, and yams. A check was made of the granaries inspected against the number of agricultural workers determined from the census to see that all had been counted. When all reports were in, the king then fixed the tax of agricultural produce, assessing each village its share of the total as a unit.

A tax, related to the number of burials performed, was levied on grave diggers. Contributions were also made to the palace by the family of the deceased. These were earmarked after a year to pay for the burial of princes, chiefs, and foreign captives who had died a natural death and had no family in Dahomey. The fee for certifying the natural death of a slave was 3,000 cowries (Burton, 1893[II]:107). Occasional references occur to ransom demanded for prisoners, and some revenue resulted from confiscatory fines and penalties. Other sources of state revenue were the taxes and tribute on subject towns, and the revenue from foreign trade.

ROYAL EQUIVALENTS

Among the duties of the king was that of proclaiming certain of the equivalents which were to prevail during his reign. There were many equivalents of a customary character in Dahomean life, such as the payments made to the bride's parents at marriage, the ritual fees to priests and various village officials on ceremonial occasions, the precisely calculated gift exchanges between kin groups at funerals, and so on. These were customary equivalents, and there is nothing to indicate that they would change from one regime to another.

The equivalents prevailing for imported goods were proclaimed by the king. Dalzel reports that Adahoonzou "issued a proclamation, that no trader should at any market pay more than thirty-two cabesses of cowries for a man and twenty-six cabesses for a woman slave. . . ." and the king himself bought slaves at this price, "he paying the price which he himself had fixed, in strung cowries, at the gate of the palace" (1793:213–15). To Commander Wilmot, the king said that his price for a slave was "80 dollars, with 4 dollars custom on each" (Burton, 1893[II]:249). Port dues also "varied with every reign" (*ibid.*:94, n.1).

The situation was somewhat different with respect to market prices. While these were usually fixed by local bodies, as we shall see in Chapter V, it was the responsibility of the king to determine the general levels which were to prevail during his reign and to make such changes as might be necessary in response to shortages or abundance of stocks. Eventually, in time of difficulty such as that which apparently prevailed during the regime of Gelele, all equivalents were raised. Indeed, Gelele seems to have instituted a kind of ten-year plan. According to Burton, "It is said that Gelele has resolved to grind the faces of his subjects for ten years of which six are now elapsed. After that time they will be supplied to honest labor, and a man shall live on a cowrie a day, so cheap will provisions become" (1893[II]:57, n.1). During these six years, equivalents had been raised fourfold. "Prices have quadrupled during the last six years," Burton says, and again, "The Cankey-ball (Dahomey's quartern loaf) fetched, under the old king, three cowries—is now worth twelve" (*ibid.*:162–63).

Equivalents in Dahomey were monetized, that is to say, expressed in cowries. Their character as proclaimed equivalents, however, was unmistakable. Not only were they officially administered, but they changed relatively infrequently and took on a customary character. This is evident, for example, in the lists of market prices reported by Forbes and others where the price of each item is given as the prevailing price for that time and place. Even the designation of the currency unit may reflect the customary equivalent, as in the well-known instance of five strings of cowries being called a "galinha," "because it was the price of a fowl" (Burton, 1893[I]:107, n.1).

Nothing in the nature of an organized labor market existed. "As Mungo Park stated in the last century," Burton observes, "paid service is unknown to the negro. Indeed, African languages ignore the word" (Burton, 1893[II]:132–33, n.2). At Whydah, in Forbes' time, canoemen and carriers, mostly strangers from other parts of the Coast, were "hired out" in work parties by their head men. "The subsistence . . . for carriers and hammockmen . . . is three strings of cowries . . . for men, and two for women, per day" (Forbes, 1851[II]:81). Though reckoned in cowries, the payments were made, at least in part, in goods—cloth, tobacco, and rum (*ibid.*[I]:122). The "load" for carriers was likewise fixed. When one of

Duncan's carriers lagged behind in traveling from Abomey to Whydah, a messenger was sent to the Prime Minister in the capital who "immediately sent fresh men with orders to punish the villains who had hung back, as, he said, he had himself examined each of their loads, and found them all considerably under the regulated weight for carriers" (1847[II]:291).

So far as the evidence indicates, there were no substitutable equivalents such as would permit the giving of one kind of goods for another in payment, e.g., in taxes. Taxes on agricultural produce were collected in kind and no provision for substitutions is reported.

Public works were also the concern of the king. Dalzel remarks that "the King summons his Caboceers and portions out the labor among them, paying their people for their trouble" (1793:xii). The state of the roads was, as we have noted, reviewed at the Annual Customs. Dalzel tells also of the king instructing his caboceers to build a road from Abomey to Whydah, providing each with a piece of string to designate the width of the road" (*ibid.*:170–71).

The king exhibited his concern for the family by his appointment of "public women." There were in Dahomey, Burton says:

public women, an organized and royal institution, appointed from the palace. . . . The present king has appointed a fresh troop of ladies of pleasure, but they have not as yet received permission to practice. (Burton, 1893[II]:148)

In this instance also the name derives from the equivalent:

At first the honorarium was twenty cowries; hence the common title "Ko-si," score-wife . . . at the representation of the ministers the solatium was increased to two strings, or fourfold. (*Ibid.*:148)

The king appointed these women to take up residence throughout the kingdom "to safeguard the peace of private families" (Norris in Dalzel, 1793:129). Norris explains that such a precaution is necessary because people of rank engrossed the major part of the women and the penalties for adultery were severe. A Dahomean man, moreover, might be required to abstain from sexual contact with his wife for as long as three years after the woman gave birth. Otherwise subsequent children, it was held, would be sickly (Herskovits, 1938[I]:268).

THE PALACE

The state sphere in Dahomey was closely tied to the royal household and its palace economy. No neat division existed, nor can it in fact be introduced between the revenues and the functions attributable to the palace on the one hand, the state on the other. Their roles were intimately connected. For this reason we have combined them under the heading of the palace economy.

The king's wives numbered, for instance, according to some estimates, about 2,000. Many of them played an important part in the administration of the state. Others were employed at various crafts. All were resident at the Abomey palace and in the king's palace at Akpueho. Also resident at the Abomey palace were many members of the Amazons, Dahomey's standing army estimated to number up to 5,000 women (Herskovits, 1938[II]:88, n.3). Other female residents of the palace included a large number of slaves at the service of the harem and the older women of the household, the latter in charge of the graves of the deceased kings. One of several estimates places the total number of women, including Amazons, at the Abomey palace itself at 3,000 to 4,000 (Dunglas, 1957:92).

Some of the king's offspring acted as special messengers and performed other duties in the king's service. Burton estimated the royal descendants to have numbered about 2,000. Le Herissé gives a much higher figure, 12,000 (Le Herissé 1911:35).

Dahomey employed an extensive state bureaucracy of ministers, administrators, auditors, toll collectors, police, and others. The chief functionaries in Abomey, although living in their own houses, were supplied with food from the king's palace (Duncan, 1847[I]:257-58).

The palace itself was an imposing structure. Each monarch erected a gateway of his own which consisted of a gap in the wall closed by rough wooden doors. Before this gate a long shed, about twenty feet in breadth and sixty feet high with a sloping thatched roof, was built alongside the wall. Here the monarch, with his court squatting around him, would recline on mats to dispense justice and perform his other royal duties. The king's plantations were one of the sources of royal revenue. These yielded palm oil and other produce. Oil and palm kernels from the king's palace at Akpueho were exported at Whydah. The king's plantations were tended by domestic slaves who had a special status and could not be sold.

Also at the Akpueho palace various crafts, such as the making of cloth and pipes, were located. Textiles for the king and other members of the royal household were woven here. Long storage sheds contained maize and other supplies. There were also dye houses and pottery works, and in all these enterprises the king's wives participated. A minor source of revenue were the elephant hunts of the Amazons. These provided not only food for feasts but bones and skulls for the fetish houses and eventually tusks and teeth for export at Whydah.

ADMINISTRATION AND DUALITY

The administration of Dahomey attained excellence in the way of honesty, precision, and reliability. Gautier (1935) rated its performance as unsurpassed among African states. Almost automatic means of check and control were employed. Operational devices were in use that offered mnemotechnical and arithmetical facilities which helped to master administrative detail. As we shall see, institutional checks of a rare effectiveness also were practiced. An original method offered in the difference of the sexes, linking officials of every grade by twos, such as male acting official and female controller. As Burton says, "Dahomean officials, male and female, high and low, are always in pairs" (1893[I]:33). In this the initiative came from above and belonged to the state sphere.

Another deeper and broader initiative sprang from the nonstate sphere and worked as a spontaneous protection of autonomy. Ancestor worship, with its shrines present in every dwelling, crowding around fetish houses, and, in even greater profusion, around cult houses present in all sib compounds, created an atmosphere of faith exerting an antibureaucratic pressure. The emotional foundations of the rule of law were thus internalized, making superfluous the governmental apparatus of constraint with the masses of the people.

The startling device of relying on the duality of sexes was carried out with thoroughness. In the royal administrative system everything went by pairs and even multiple pairs. First of all, every official in the kingdom had his female counterpart, or "mother," resident in the royal compound. Within the palace, then, the king had a complete counterpart of the administrative apparatus throughout the kingdom. These women officials were called *naye*. It was the duty of each woman to know intimately all the administrative affairs of her male counterpart and to keep constant check upon his operations. Herskovits gives an illustration how it worked:

For example, it may be supposed that one of these *naye* was entrusted with remembering the previous reports of the *Yovoga* who, being in command of the sea districts, controlled all the makers of salt. The particular *naye* to whom the *Yovoga* reported would be spoken of as the *Yovogano*, the "mother of the *Yovoga*," and she was always present whenever the question of the production of salt was brought up at court councils. She already had in her possession the report of the independent officers sent by the King to survey the salt industry, and it was her task to see that the *Yovoga's* statement of operations corresponded to this other when he made his accounting. . . . It was the stated policy of the King to listen to none of his officials unless he first called for the *naye* who was the "mother" of this chief. (1938[I]:111)

Another group of women, the *kposi* or "wives of the leopard," were in command of the *naye*. There were likewise two groups of *kposi*: one, consisting of eight women, always present when the king held audience with his counselors; a second group, similarly of eight, which over and above stood in attendance when ministers or priests reported. In this way there existed three sets of witnesses to statements of an important official—his "mother," the eight *kposi* who were always present, and the other eight specialist witnesses called in when particular ministers made their report.

Dual organization existed also throughout the army. The army was divided into two wings, the right and the left, and within each wing into a male and female part. Every male, from the highest ranking officer down to the last soldier, had his female counterpart in the palace. The right wing, for example, was commanded by the Mingan, or prime minister of Dahomey, and his counterpart was the "She-Mingan, (who being within the palace, takes precedence of him" (Burton, 1893[I]:146).

Forbes says of the army:

Considered as an army, it is in two brigades, the *miegan's* and the *mayo's*, the right and the left. . . . In the right, there are two *miegans* and two *agaous*, a male and an amazon; and the same equivalent rank is carried down to the private in each brigade, male and female. These relationships in military rank are called father and mother; and . . . the male soldier, when accused, appeals to his "mother" to speak for him. (Cf. Herskovits, 1938[II]:84)

All visitors to the court at Abomey were assigned a "mother" who looked after their needs during their stay and who was present at all audiences granted to the guest of the king.

The new king upon his succession to the throne retained the ministers who served his father, but appointed younger men of high rank as his own representatives. This served the purpose of training the younger men in their duties while at the same time providing a check upon the elder statesmen.

Provinces incorporated into Dahomey were permitted to retain their own administration if they had voluntarily submitted, but a man from the king's court, called a "king's wife," might be sent to reside with the local caboceer and exercise surveillance over his affairs on behalf of the king.

In the house of each minister lives a King's daughter and two officers: these superintend the minister's trade, on which he pays tribute according to their report. If a dispute arises in which the King's interest is at stake, these officers report direct; and if the dispute is serious, the minister is arrested or fined. (Forbes, 1851[I]:34–35)

There is, of course, a paradox in talking about a reduction of bureaucratism in view of the type of duality which doubled and quadrupled the numbers of officialdom. Yet the fact cannot be gainsaid that all responsible observers, friendly or otherwise, are agreed in acknowledging the Dahomeans' outstanding efficiency in civil and military affairs.

One cannot ignore the possibility that a sociological element was at work, namely, a predominance of female characteristics. We refuse to attempt to appraise the relative weight of the physical and the cultural factors that might have been operative. The fact is that in very few communities of state level were women called upon to play so large a part in services vital to functioning of the polity. The gifts of the female sex for absorbing detail, retaining information on facts of everyday life in which commonsense is anchored, have been tested and not found wanting.

The recognized excellence of administration and the eminent role played in it by the female element does not seem fully to account for the extent to which Dahomean women were drawn into public life up to its highest levels. This suggests that behind the duality device as such there must have been active some motivation stemming from a mental attitude that transcended considerations of practical efficiency.

Duality was indeed a pervasive feature of the Dahomean culture. The tissue of officialdom was extended not only vertically as a hierarchy but also horizontally by additions on the same level. Symmetry, comprising all organs of the state from the body of the field army down to its least unit, could scarcely exist unless it was due to an ingrained culture trait. The predilection for twos left its stamp on the semantics of kinship, the organization of the pantheon, and the order of everyday soothsaying. This pursuance of a dual notion extending from the cosmos to the microcosm of the community did not stop even at the person of the monarch. Kingship itself was "twin." The king had a double role as Bush King and as Town King. Burton describes the fact:

One of the Dahomean monarch's peculiarities is, that he is a double . . . two in one. Gelele, for instance, is King of the city, Adde-kpon of the "bush"; that is to say, of the farmer folk and the country as opposed to the city. (1893[II]:58)

The Bush King had a duplicate of the environment which existed for the Town King: there was a palace set aisde for him only six miles southwest of Abomey with a corps of officials duplicating those of the Town King; in the army organization, the Bush King had his captains, male and female; the Annual Customs of the Town King were followed by a repetition of the Annual Customs for the Bush King; and there was a "mother" for the Bush King as well as for the Town King. As Skertchly says, "whatever is done for the king (Gelele) in public is thrice repeated; first for the Amazons, then for Adde-kpon, and thirdly, for Adde-kpon's Amazons" (1874:271).

Actually, a veritable obsession with the perfection of duality prevailed from the earliest mythological notions of a metaphysical order down to the domestic predilection for twin births. The liking for an ample progeniture may have induced this bent. A statistical frequency of twins might explain the conventional preference attaching to offspring born proximately to twins, whether after, before, or between pairs of twins.

At the head of the Dahomean pantheon was the dual divinity of *Mawu-Lisa*. "The ideal type of every group in the divine world," Mercier says, "is a pair of twins of opposite sex, or more rarely, of the same sex" (Mercier, 1954c:231). He refuses to follow up the cultural interpretation of the androgynous element in the cult of twins, preferring to turn to the sphere of political organization "in which duality is immediately apparent" (*ibid.*:232). He obviously has in mind the institution of the Bush King, the *economic* importance of which he was the first to recognize. "The dual monarchy," he says, "did not perpetuate itself, until it was revealed to Gezo that the prosperity of Dahomey depended on its revival. Thus Gezo installed Gapke and Gelele, Addokpon and everything that was done for the one had also to be done for the other" (*ibid.*:232). Thus the nineteenth century re-enacted the ancient story of King Akaba and his twin sister Xãgba "who ruled jointly, in accordance with the doctrine that twins must always be treated alike" (*ibid.*:232).

We now turn to the question of the economic function of the Bush King with his seat in Kana. In Dalzel's time Kana was a large town, about eight miles from Abomey, numbering some 15,000 inhabitants. Quoting Norris, he wrote: "The king frequently resides here, and has a spacious house which occupies with its appendages almost as much ground as St. James's Park: it is enclosed with a high mud wall, which forms nearly a square" (Dalzel, 1793:118–19). Norris measured one side of it and found it one thousand seven hundred paces long. (This was about an English mile, the editor of Norris remarks in a footnote.) "Halfway between Kana and Abomey is a country house of the King's called Dawhee the ancient residence of the family and a capital of their little territory, before they emerged from their original obscurity" (Dalzel, 1793:120). The countryside of Calmina—an earlier name for Kana—was very fertile and its crops sustained the neighboring towns.

Kana contained a royal burial place and one of the oldest and largest marketplaces of the country. It grew from the family's favorite resort and burial place into the residence of the shadow government and court, as well as into a separate economic capital. Since Dahomey's redistributive economy was transacted in kind, the Bush King's palace had an important function of its own. It was a storage and industrial center, housing a large volume of crops collected as taxes and distributing them together with manufactured items.

The separation from the royal court at Abomey of the productive and distributive economic activities focused on Kana may have been a convenient procedure and even necessary from the administrative, the military, and the technological angles.

At his Dawhee palace, halfway between Abomey and Kana, the king was only an hour's distance by a landscaped and perfectly built road from both his political and his economic capital. Treasure goods were guarded and cared for in the Simbony Palace, i.e., Great House, at Abomey. These included cowries, iron bars, clothes, arms, ammunition, and some articles of European furniture. Provisions for the king's numerous family were kept here. Wives for substantial young men against sums of up to 20,000 cowries were delivered at the gates of the treasure house at the political capital. Raw materials for the blacksmiths who produced arms and tools, payment in kind to diverse craftsmen, building materials for fortifications, gates, walls, bridges, and strategic highways were distributed.

The permanent danger was Oyo. Since 1712 a heavy tribute, the *agban,* at times increased at short notice under threat of a devastating cavalry incursion, was a source of anguish to Dahomey. The *agban* was annually delivered at Kana to the Oyo delegation. Several incidents show the unreliability of the surrounding tribes in spite of the proximity of the capital. Several times the king had to pacify the area to protect the royal cemetery and the peace of the market. Since ancient times a Yoruba settlement had existed in Kana which, after the disastrous defeat of the Dahomeans, acted as an intermediary between Dahomey and the Oyo conquerors in negotiating the tribute. Forty-one cases, each containing 41 guns, formed part of the *agban.* It was understandable if the munition at least was kept well away.

CHAPTER FOUR

*R*eciprocity: Mutual Aid and Cooperation

The redistributive pattern in the economy of the state sphere had many ramifications, as we have seen. In its day-to-day aspect, however, livelihood was embedded in state-free institutions of neighborhood, kinship, and worship, all of which were local.

The productive resources of society had to be drawn upon regularly from outside the family and the sib. They were needed to prepare a field in case the owner was sick, to build mud walls, to thatch roofs, and to provide small cattle for sacrifice, food for ceremonial occasions, and meals for weddings, burials, or mourning rituals. Clearly these tasks often surpassed the strength of the individual householders. How, in the absence of a pool of available labor for hire, was labor channeled to fulfill these needs? In the nonstate sphere this was brought about through one of the country's main institutions—the *dokpwe*, or labor team. Even public works, such as the building of roads or repairing the walls of the palace, were at times carried out by the *dokpwe*, though these came under the jurisdiction of the state sphere with its redistributive system. The king in such a case called upon his caboceers or upon the *dokpwega*, the chief of the *dokpwe*, to summon their men for the emergency. The king, like any host, would be expected to provide feasts for the work party and give presents to the leaders.

The *dokpwe* was not the only, though it was certainly the major, cooperative body to supply ubiquitous assistance. Reciprocity, i.e., the principle underlying its practice, was as essential a feature in the economic life of the nonstate sphere redistribution was in the economy of the state. Together with householding, reciprocity was the main economic pattern in the nonstate sphere.

An attitude of mutual goodwill often accompanies reciprocity. But attitude alone, whether of cooperation or competition, cannot organize the economy. More essential are the institutions, such as the market, that channel the process and provide support for those attitudes. This is obvious also for some famous types of primitive reciprocating. Mutuality is acted out between symmetrical parts of a family group in the subsistence organization of the Trobrianders (Malinowski, 1922), or in the multiple marriages of the Banaro of New Guinea (Thurnwald, 1916), or in the simple exchange marriages of the Tiv of West Africa (P. Bohannan, 1954:69–75; L. and P. Bohannan, 1957:72 ff.).

Where symmetrical traits occur in the social structure, mutuality behavior occurs with ease. A different source of mutuality was identified by Aristotle: the good will that inheres in any community, without which community cannot be said to obtain, and finds its expression in a readiness to share burdens. In either case there is a supporting structural element: symmetry in the one, the active good will among members of a definite community in the other. Aristotle's *koinonia* implies, however, a much wider range of mutuality than that suggested by the correspondence between symmetrically structured groups. *Koinonia* may obtain in a small group or it may prevail throughout the entire society. Whether small or large, the community in which it exists, may combine redistribution of goods between its members with a sharing of the burdens of labor "in turn." The underlying principle he called reciprocity (*antipeponthos*).

The main institution allocating labor in Dahomey was the *dokpwe*. Organized in a pattern of reciprocating labor teams, the *dokpwe* formed part of a powerful structure of aid comprising, among other institutions, the *so* (craft guild) and the *gbe* (mutual aid group). The latter institution channeled mutual aid in goods, the former institution being chiefly concerned with labor.

WORK TEAMS

"Every Dahomean man must know three things well: How to cut a field, how to build a wall, and how to roof a house" (Herskovits, 1938[I]:30). This popular saying reflected the three major tasks in which a Dahomean might be called upon to participate by virtue of reciprocity.

How in fact was such labor channeled or allocated in Dahomey in the absence of a labor market, i.e., where wage labor was unknown? The *dokpwe*, or labor team, was a universal institution in Dahomey.* It contrasted sharply in its objectives and operations with the labor market of Western societies and was devoted to the fulfillment of the tasks of the community, such as ensuring the cultivation of the fields and assisting in carrying out the material obligations of marriage and the obligations to parents. In this way labor was organized in a pattern of compulsory mutual aid or reciprocity.

All full-fledged Dahomeans of a village belonged to the *dokpwe*. The community-wide character of the institution is expressed in the comment of a Dahomean chief:

It is for everyone; whether you are a chief or a common man, the *dokpwe* will help you. If you need a house, it will build one for you; if you have a field to cultivate, it will break your ground. When you are sick it helps you; when you die, it buries you. Every man must show respect for the head of the *dokpwe;* when he comes here, I take off my chief's cap to him. (Herskovits, 1938[I]:64)

Should a poor man and a chief both request the help of the *dokpwe*, it was said that help would be given strictly in the order in which the request had been made.

The *dokpwega*, or head of the *dokpwe*, was the third official of the village, ranking below the chief and his assistant. In a large village there might be a *dokpwe*, with its headman, in

* The author who realized the economic importance of this institution is Herskovits (1938) whose presentation we follow in this chapter.

each quarter; in smaller villages one would suffice for the entire village. The *dokpwega* had three assistants to help him in the execution of his duties. Obedience to the call of the *dokpwega* was unquestioned in all nonpolitical aspects of life and was enforced by strict sanctions:

No man would without serious cause refuse to obey the call of the *dokpwega*. Should he do so without permission, he would be ostracized by his fellow-villagers, his wives would leave him, and his family, punished because of his offence, would become poor. Neither he nor any of his relatives could obtain burial. . . . (*ibid.*:70)

According to tradition, even the king was subject to call by the *dokpwe*. On one occasion, during the reign of Gelele,

this powerful King with his drummers, his hammock bearers, and his numerous suite passed a *dokpwe* at work without pausing to greet the *dokpwega*. At once the *dokpwega*, staff in hand, halted the procession, and demanding of Gelele why he had violated the rule of the *dokpwe*, summoned him to work in the field. The story goes that Gelele made apologies, explained that he had not noticed the *dokpwe*, and offered as a penance to send fifty slaves to work. The *dokpwega*, however, was not satisfied, and that night assessed Gelele a fine of many cases of rum and numerous cloths. (*ibid.*:70–71)

This semilegendary incident reflects the scope and character of this institution in the minds of the Dahomeans. Herskovits offers a further illustration of the relationship between the king and *dokpwe*. In building a road ordered by a king, it was said that the *dokpwega* of the district where the royal residence was located would call the king to work as a member of the *dokpwe* to which he belonged. When the king received the message, he would send food and drink for the men and provide sufficient manpower to complete the road by calling out his army.

The *dokpwe* rendered aid to all Dahomeans to fulfill certain personal obligations and to meet emergencies in specified situations. There were five distinct occasions on which the *dokpwe* acted. The *dokpwe* ensured that the fields of a villager were cultivated in case he were incapacitated. If he were ill or too old to do the hard labor of breaking his fields for planting and had no one to aid him, the *dokpwe* came to his assistance. If

the man were poor, he need not feed the workers nor pay a fee
to the *dokpwega*. The aid which he himself had rendered to
others in his youth, or, if a young man, would render again in
the future, fulfilled the obligation of reciprocity.

The second type of assistance was rendered to a man whose
fields were too extensive to be cultivated by his own labor and
the labor at his disposal. In such a case, the man summoned the
dokpwe by presenting to its chief a stipulated payment (in
modern times, a bottle of spirits, four yards of cloth, and two
francs fifty centimes) and provided a feast for the workers on
as lavish a scale as he could afford.

The *dokpwe* was also called upon to assist a man in fulfilling
the traditional obligation to his wife's parents, the *asitogle*.
Under this arrangement, a son-in-law had to complete an
important piece of work for his father-in-law every year or so
and keep his mother-in-law's house in good repair. Dahomeans
held that, "A man who has many daughters is a rich man"
(*ibid.*:73). Should the son-in-law neglect his duties, his wife
eventually would be taken away from him and returned to the
household of her parents. If a man had many wives, the obligation became onerous, if not impossible; and the *dokpwe* was
called upon to help. In one case, it is reported, the *dokpwe*
from the son-in-law's village traveled 45 kilometers to build a
compound wall for the father-in-law in Abomey.

Likewise, the *dokpwe* could be called upon to help a man in
the services owing to his father. Until the age of twenty or
twenty-five, even though a son may have acquired his own
fields, he was obliged to work on his father's fields until he had
established his own household and might even continue to
assist his father later as a courtesy. Again, if the son had sufficient means, he would pay the customary fee. If not, his fellow
villagers worked for him at no cost to himself, subject only to
his obligation when called upon to help them in turn through
the *dokpwe*.

Finally, upon the death of every Dahomean the *dokpwe* was
summoned to wrap the corpse in its burial cloths and to take
charge of the elaborate funeral ceremonies.

Work parties were a festive occasion. Work songs were sung and there was a feast at the completion of the task. At some tasks, such as thatching a roof, men worked in pairs. If only one *dokpwe* was called, it was divided into two parts, the one competing against the other.

The office of *dokpwega* was one of trust, and the *dokpwega* himself was a man of high standing. The post was hereditary, and each *dokpwega*, in the presence of the king or a chief of royal blood, named the son who was to be his successor. The ceremonial installation of a new *dokpwega* took place in the king's presence at the royal palace and was attended by the members of the court and the family of the new *dokpwega*.

CRAFT GUILDS

The societies of craftsmen provided numerous examples of reciprocity in work arrangements. Working "in turns" was the usual practice among blacksmiths and weavers and often among potters as well. Workers in iron, cloth, and pottery were organized into a cooperative society called a *so*, under the direction of a head called *soga*. (Blacksmiths and weavers belonged in any case to family groups.) The practice was for all members of the *so* to work on the raw material of each member in turn, the blacksmiths producing hoes and axes, and the weavers, cloth, which was then sold by the individual members who supplied the raw material. Pottery was fired cooperatively. Should a man fail to observe his obligations to the group, he was subject to being disciplined by the members.

Cooperative work societies which gave assistance in cultivating the fields of their members were also known as *so*. This society did not conflict with the *dokpwe*, for any group of men might bind themselves together for such a purpose as long as five or more men working together had the permission of the *dokpwega*. A distinction between the *so* and the *dokpwe* was, however, maintained.

. . . when the members of a . . . [*so*] wish to help one of their number till his fields, they ask a *dokpwega* to preside over the work. It is understood, however, that even though he does direct this work, it is not a *dokpwe,* but a *so* that is performing. (*ibid.:*253)

The *so,* and the *gbe* (discussed below), provided assistance to its members in time of need. Should a member fall ill, his fellows came to work for him. Members paid dues and stipulated amounts were given on the occasion of the death of relatives. The *so* participated in the funeral of a member, and in cases of hardship assessments were levied on members to provide for the family of the deceased.

Women who sold foodstuffs in the market belonged to similar societies called *sodudo.* These differed from the guilds in that they did not control the organization of work but had mutual aid functions similar to the *so* and *gbe.*

FAMILIAL AID

One of the most widespread institutions in Dahomey was the mutual aid society, called *gbe;* this name was also given to the extended family. It was a voluntary association whose members were bound in blood-brotherhood to help one another in the performance of certain obligations, as well as meeting for various social occasions. The obligations and the amount of the contribution each member would be called upon to make were stipulated in advance upon formation of the society. Aid was given when a member fell ill or suffered a considerable monetary loss, or on those ceremonial occasions when a member was obligated to make large outlays in gifts, as at the funeral of a parent-in-law. Herskovits describes one such ceremonial occasion:

On the morning after the actual interment of the body, each man married or betrothed to a daughter of the dead brings his *gbe* to aid him in making the gifts which the occasion demands. (*ibid.:*251)

A piece of black cloth "in silk or velvet" together with money is presented to a man's wife or his future wife.

After he has proffered these two cloths, the man turns to the members of his society who are gathered behind him and says, "Now I am on my way. Push me!" This is the time when the fellow-members of his society must give the amounts agreed upon when the society was formed. (*ibid.:* 251)

Ceremonial gift exchanges were competitive. A man without a *gbe* could not gain the prestige that attended a lavish display. His wife or betrothed also had her *gbe* at hand. The competition was enhanced as, in turn, sons-in-law and daughters of the deceased engaged in this gift exchange between the man's party and the woman's party. Any member who was unable to make his contribution when called upon was advanced the necessary funds from the common treasury of the society. When in a position to do so he would repay this sum.

When a member died the *gbe* assisted at the funeral, providing a shroud sewn together from the pieces of cloth given by each member.

The *gbe* had a set of four officials and drums and banners which were displayed at public appearances. Women's societies were often richer than those of the men.

THE BEST FRIEND

The "best friend" was a relationship entailing not only confidence but obligations which the best friend performed throughout his lifetime. It was the best friend to whom a man confided his will and who acted as executor for his estate. The relationship is illustrated in the case of a man who would be forced to call upon his best friend to help him in making a marriage. Thus, when the girl's family

asks help of their daughter's fiance, or later, of their son-in-law he goes to his friend, who gives him whatever is necessary. . . . When the girl has been brought to her husband's compound, her husband's friend provides her with firewood and, when he comes from the field, he gives her maize and millet. If she becomes ill it is this man, not her husband, who cares for her. (*ibid.:*313)

Even the best friend's family was involved. If a daughter was born to the marriage she was pledged as wife to the best friend. If for some reason the man could not fulfill this obligation, it fell upon his son to supply a woman from his family to be wife to the son of his father's best friend. So compelling was this obligation upon the second generation that should the prospective bride elope with another before the marriage was consummated a crisis ensued. The man to whom the girl had been promised would go to the head of his sib who then pronounced a general divorce between all the women of that sib who were married to men of the sib to which the eloped girl belonged. That same night these women would be sent for, wherever they might be living. This action would have repercussions throughout the country, since the extended families of the sibs might reside in different parts of Dahomey. The men whose wives were thus taken from them instituted a search for the girl and brought her, together with her parents, before the sib head. When the girl had been forced to announce the name of her seducer, the sib head again proclaimed a divorce, this time between all the women of the sib who were married to men of the sib to which the offending male belonged. Negotiations between the sibs involved in such an affair often took many months, and the king himself might be called in to mediate the dispute.

No matter how the dispute was settled, however, the girl was not given to the man to whom she had been pledged. Instead, and apparently in the interest of keeping the peace, she was given to a man not related to any sib involved in the affair. The injured man, however, received the most eligible young girl in her sib as a wife. Prior promises that may have been made in regard to this girl were overridden, for the settlement of this obligation assumed first importance. Only after this settlement had been reached did the sib heads revoke the wholesale divorce decrees upon all members of the sibs involved.

THE PAWN

These relationships of mutual aid helped to assure the Dahomean against falling into a state of dependency. Should an occasion arise, however, when these procedures were inadequate, another type of reciprocity was invoked—the giving of pawns. If a man suffered a misfortune, such as incurring a heavy fine which he did not have the means to pay, he might obtain the necessary funds from another, giving one of his children as pawn in return. The honorable character of the relationship is suggested by the fact that a slave could not be offered as a pawn.

Meticulous safeguards surrounded this institution. The agreement was transacted in the presence of the village chief, when the sum of money was handed over and a date set for its repayment. No interest was charged; the pawn worked for the lender during the period. Children too young to work were not acceptable. At the end of the set time both parties appeared again before the chief, when pawn and money were returned.

If the debtor could not redeem the pawn at the appointed time, an extension was granted. If the delay was too protracted and the pawn a girl, she might be taken as wife by the lender. The money was then regarded as equivalent to the usual monetary obligations which must be fulfilled by a prospective son-in-law for certain types of marriage. The lender with his pawn would appear before the village chiefs of his own and the debtor's village who would then certify the marriage. If the pawn were a son, however, three alternatives existed. First, the debtor might agree to double the sum and place a second son with the lender, setting a new date for the repayment. Or again, a second son would be given, but the lender must then specify certain work which was to be done to discharge the debt, e.g., the number of rows to be hoed on his fields. In this case, the debtor might call upon the *dokpwe* to help him complete the work in discharge of the debt. As a third course, the two chiefs of the villages concerned might determine a given amount of work for the pawn to complete in order to discharge the debt and the amount of time the work required. When this time had elapsed, the debt was considered discharged, regardless of the actual work at which the pawn had been engaged.

Public opinion turned against a person who abused a pawn, since this was an institution to which all might at some time resort. Other procedures covered the case of either the creditor or debtor dying before the pawn was redeemed.

CHAPTER FIVE

*H*ouseholding:
*L*and and *R*eligion

PLANTATION AND PEASANT PLOT

The economic foundation of nonagricultural society is to be found in particular ecological balances. With agriculture land moves into a central position; livelihood and social organization are related to the agricultural setting, be it tribal or familial. The economic pattern in such societies is householding. The movement of goods is directed by the householder, who both allocates the labor of the household and apportions the food to be consumed. Hence, in regions of rainfall tillage the *oikos*, as the Greeks called the "house," becomes a permanent and fixed social institution. Aristotle said the *oikos* consisted of the family and the slaves. About five centuries earlier Hesiod had pictured it in a similar way, adding that unless food was stored for the winter, the family might face starvation.

First among the forms of land tenure in Dahomey rank the king's domains, worked by prisoners of war, to which may be added areas held by the princes. These big estates (*gletanu*) engage in the wholesale production of staple foods that are retailed by market women. At the other extreme are the villagers' plots, owned by the subjected aboriginals—former slaves, still bound to devote, at the chief's bidding, half of their working day to the tasks that fall as a public duty to the local administration.

THE SIB AND THE COMPOUND

The traditional form of land tenure in Dahomey centers on

the compound, an agglomeration of huts and buildings occupied by an extended family (*gbe*), which is itself based on a group of agnatically related men who are close kinsmen through common membership in the patrilineal lineage or sib (*xenu*). Melville Herskovits (1938[I]:137 ff.), whose work provides the data of this chapter, has called attention to the ways in which this form of settlement is interlocked with the sib and especially with its religious organization.

The lands held by members of the fifty sibs, each broken up into many compounds and associated fields, rank in size between *gletanu* and the villagers' plots. In this sense "sib compounds" may be regarded as "middle class" holdings, a term otherwise scarcely appropriate to land that is subject to succession and entail.

A collectivity of from two to five compounds forms neither a mere association of individuals nor does it represent a communal holding linked by indissoluble bonds of kinship and religion. In Dahomey such a grouping of dwellings forms part of the ancestral home of a sib which had been settled over several generations in close proximity, following religiously sanctified rules of interment and succession. The completed settlement houses a family associated with a branch of a descent group of sib. Its members look to the particular compound in which the founder lies buried as their ancestral shrine. The external requisite of such a rural development is a range of available land into which the additional compounds can expand. The internal requisite is acceptance of the religious injunction binding on sib members not to leave the founder's tomb unattended by a male descendant. After the incumbent's death, his family must leave again the ancestral compound to make room for the next in succession. Sib succession is primarily by ramification, i.e., brothers following one upon the other by age before the next generation succeeds by primogeniture, i.e., starting with the eldest son of the eldest brother. This is complemented by rules which provide for the erection of further compounds and the reburial and enshrinement of all the successors of the founder each in his own family compound.

To place the compound in the frame of the African world, we must realize that as a pattern of dwellings it is a feature of the landscape in parts of West and Sudanese Africa. But as the ancestral home of a sib and the scene of its elaborate religious practices, perhaps nowhere in Africa is the compound more intensely alive than in Dahomey.

Three features are therefore fused here. Physically and visually, the compound is a group of houses or huts surrounded by a wall or pile of great durability. With its tilled plots and clusters of palm-oil trees, the compound is a feature of the Dahomean countryside. Secondly, the compound houses the extended family (*gbe*), the male members of which are closely related—usually through a common patrilineal grandfather or great-grandfather. These same male members are associated with a sib, of which some fifty are on record. The sibs are not localized, but all sibs focus on the founding collectivity that harbors their ancestral compound. Third, and basically, the sib—to which the extended families and households are thus attached in a fundamental way—is produced and maintained by an inner religious force of rarely surpassed richness and strength. It is a form of ancestor worship that merges the habitational unit or compound and the kinship unit into an unbreakable social entity.

The economic historian cannot but be reminded of other, non-African types of rural formations, designated as manor or seigniory. Indeed, the African and West European formation have in common that these aspects are found linked: solidly walled dwellings, hereditary ranking of families, and traditional religious ideologies. This is the politicoeconomic pattern vaguely described as "feudal," a term often employed to bridge the cultural gap between tribal and knightly civilizations. Peasant household and manorial economy differed mainly in size. However, the African compound is not fortified and has no military character whatsoever; its walls ensure privacy, not security. Neither has the sib any affinity to cavalry, war chariots, or other knightly arms involving a specialized leisure class training of an elite connotation; nor does the compound carry socioeconomic ruling class privileges that imply disposal over dependent labor. These social criteria of Western feudalism are, then, strikingly absent. Thus, in spite of their common traits, a sharp contrast obtains between the manorial, feudal system of Europe and the African system of sib compounds.

Another institutional cognate to the sib compound that nevertheless manifests a strong divergence is the Dahomean monarchy. The monarchy in Dahomey is the apex of the state sphere, which is consistently separated from the tissue of local institutions existing outside of the state. The sibs and their compounds are among the latter.

We cannot fail to note a number of traits that the settled sibs on a local and modest scale have in common with the monarchy itself. And yet, what an abysmal contrast in human values! The sib, too, is a kinship body, passionately devoted to the worship of the ancestors, that manifests itself from the care for the neglected spirits and ghosts of the dead to a nationwide discipline of religious practices. The monarchy was imbued with these same values. Nothing, however, could be more different than is the domestic, humane atmosphere of the sibs from the monarch's indulgence in cruel torture on a monstrous scale, justified on grounds of reasons of state combined with the rigidly observed precepts of ancestor worship. The same virtues and values that flourished in the sib compounds underwent a moral alienation in the range of the state. The ruling dynasty also stressed its status as a sib, indeed, a supersib, claiming Allada, where the royal enstoolments were held, as its ancestral town. But while the sibs as such were invested with no constitutional prerogatives over the common villagers, the monarchy derived unlimited social and political authority from descent.

SUCCESSION AND INHERITANCE

The compound must appear as an elaborate and remarkable institution. Activated by a few simple rules of succession, a structure of great durability evolved. Once the founding gesture—an individual's act—has taken place, its effects prevail over deep-seated forces of resistance, the clinging to accustomed habitation, the personal preferences and habits. No vanities or passions shall defeat the moral law which must be upheld so that the institution may live. Traditionally sanctioned succession operates with an all-round maturity.

The founder of a new compound usually is a younger man who has wandered off his ancestral compound. He tills a portion of land, plants some oil palms, and builds a house for himself as well as one for his wife or wives. In course of time he adds a house for his sons—we assume he has two—and the daughters stay in the house of their mothers. When the sons grow up and marry they build houses in separate courtyards. A wall about twelve feet high is eventually erected around this group of houses. The founder's compound now has reached full stature. So long as he lives, this state of affairs continues unchanged. At his death a move starts which is re-enacted every time the head of the ancestral compound dies, for the house of the founder must always be occupied by the male in succession who will tend the founder's tomb which is enshrined next to the house. After the founder dies, his eldest son moves up, together with his family. At his death the successor moves into the founder's house, with his family. The wives and children of the deceased must quit the ancestral compound and remove into a new, as yet nonexistant second compound. The burden of building this compound falls on the new head of the family. Here the body of the late compound head is reburied, to be tended by one of his sons. Succession thereupon changes to primogeniture. The eldest son of the elder son now likewise is obliged to build a new compound—the third. This contingency is not repeated if the founder had only two sons. For now any successor will, upon his death, be buried near his own father's tomb in his own compound.

While the ancestral compound does not, of course, grow in size, the second and third compounds do and eventually split in two parts. At this point succession undergoes a radical change, the eldest member of the collectivity succeeding.

Thus succession evolves a master unit of kinship structure, the compound. In disregarding inheritance—in any case a minor feature in the compound—the singularity of sib tenure becomes apparent. It is, as we said, distinct from individual property and from communal ownership as well. Land can neither be freely alienated, nor is its use subject to collective decisions. The conflicting property rights as between the members of the sib that result from succession are largely resolved by the existence of separate compounds. Difficulties still may cluster around the conjunction of the two principles of transference brought about by death in the sib, namely, succession and inheritance, the one referring to status and office, the other and subordinate one, to ownership of property. Inheritance is subordinate to succession because of the purpose to which inherited possessions are devoted. Such possessions are used to defray sib contributions to cult house and other expenditures that in the last resort serve the status interest of the sib.

The line that normally separates succession and inheritance in the sib compound is here blurred by overruling principles that encompass both. Among these principles are: the identity of the name of the founder must be maintained; property must not leave the family; the elder does not inherit from the younger; females do not inherit from the male parent. Other valid principles already mentioned are ramification and primogeniture, the latter being subordinate to the former; trusteeship over palm-oil trees in favor of the sib; systematic reburials so that the deceased's own son finally comes to rest at his father's side; the establishment of a cult house within the collectivity, belonging to all of it.

The rules under which property is repartitioned and accumulated in the compound secure that neither fragmentation nor engrossing of property ensues. Rather, an impressive permanence of family possessions results, accompanied by utmost solidity of status. For not so much property as an even status level is maintained through the interlaced action of the rules of succession and inheritance. The key to this lies in the entailing effect of trusteeship and inalienability as practiced in the collectivity of compounds.

In regard to land, inheritance was merely transfer of use, not of property. This rule was an extension of the principle according to which the king alone possessed the fullness of property rights in Dahomey, whether over land or people. Hence the "owners" of land were not entitled to sell it, nor were the "owners" of slaves entitled to sell them without the king's permission. Alongside this universal inalienability was the widespread institution of trusteeship that secured the revenue of the land for definite familial ends. These were largely status requirements such as prestige representation of the head of the compound and emergency expenditures on behalf of the sib: fines, ransom, dowries, or other calamitous sums to be defrayed.

ANCESTOR WORSHIP AND CULT HOUSE

"The ancestral cult must be regarded as the focal point of Dahomean social organization. In order that a sib and its component parts may exist and be perpetuated, the worship of its ancestors must be scrupulously carried out" (Herskovits, 1938[I]:194). The linkage between the sib compound as a dwelling and settlement and as the embodiment of a national religion could not have been better expressed than in these words of Herskovits.

To go to the heart of the matter, two operational traits of the ancestral cult should be brought to mind: an intense preoccupation with the physical location of the father's tomb and a deification of deceased kin not too many years after death. The Dahomean sib in two ways united the living and the dead

—preserving the dead bodily among the living, and keeping them as gods in everyday life.

Before the labor of clearing a new field is undertaken (again following Herskovits) the farmer must ascertain what supernatural beings watch over the new land. He takes

a sample of its soil to his diviner, who, as a first formality throws the palm kernels to consult Fate whether the new ground may be cultivated. If the answer is favourable, a sacrifice to the Earth is then made, wherein the suppliant, taking earth from the projected field, moulds it into a human head with caury-shells for eyes, and placing this head on the ground offers it palm-oil, the blood of a chicken, and finally maize mixed with flour and water. This ceremony is performed while he is alone in the field, and the figure is left there to disintegrate. . . . The diviner calls separately on the various gods until one of them is designated by Destiny as the field's tutelary spirit. (*Ibid.*:31)

In this instance it is assumed that the spirit is

a powerful deity of the ancestral cult believed to reside in great trees. The man who is to work the field will then name for his diviner the great trees found upon the land, and the diviner proceeds to discover the one sheltering the spirit, which then becomes the shrine of the protecting deity. (*ibid.*:21)

The owner pours palm oil over the trunk of the tree as a libation and repeats this offering every fourth day. From time to time he adds a chicken. He now

may begin the preparation, and later the cultivation of his field, but during this period, and also later when the crops are being harvested he continues his weekly libations of palm oil and awaits signs which will indicate whether the spirit of the field is a well-intentioned one. (*Ibid.*:32)

If, in spite of these offerings, there is ill luck in the family, or, most important of all, if yields turn out poor,

he sees in this a demonstration that the spirit is unfriendly, and, after consultation with his diviner, the field may be abandoned.

When for five or six years a field produces good crops, and the owner prospers, it is his obligation to visit a priest of the cult of the guardian spirit of the field, and from him to ascertain the type of ritual necessary to "establish" this spirit as a beneficent "public" deity. (*Ibid.*:32)

The owner now builds for the spirit a small shelter around the trunk of the tree, and from this time on, unless he is a priest of this particular spirit,

he may himself not sacrifice to it, but must summon a priest of the cult to offer his sacrifices for him. The tree itself becomes communal property, and any one is permitted to worship at the shrine erected at its base. . . . (*Ibid.:32*)

Analyzing the process by which a single tree in a tilled field of a compound comes to grow into a public shrine illustrates the significant merging of sib and organized worship in Dahomey. Eventually, the sib erects a cult house, a site of worship and training, appointing one of its members to hereditary priesthood, and subsisting a number of its novitiates over the years. The god takes over the protection of the sib and imbues its collectivities with the spirit of the deity.

Dahomean religion sprouted from three pantheons of great gods of a broad mythological background. Hierarchies of priests lived in cult houses devoted to gods who belonged to one of the circles. Around the official priesthood swarms of diviners practiced prophecy and kept the believers in touch with Destiny by means of *fa,* a popular system of divination. The diviner employed everyday magic for prophecy as the most common means of advising. *Fa* was as good as a home medicine in the religious practice. It kept a man in touch with his Destiny: a variant of Fate which is not wholly unapproachable to ordinary man. The layman also can acquire some knowledge of *fa* and explore his Destiny himself. A more stable belt of devotees appealed to the priests to be initiated into the cult, which involved many months of training, instruction in formal dances, the acquiring of one or two cult languages together with the esoteric knowledge common to the novitiates. The priesthood was attached to the sib which established the cult house and appointed the initiating priest. The cult house, set up close to the sib's ancestral compound, was permanently provided with sustenance from there.

Numbers of initiates were also taken care of by the patron

sib. The stages of initiation marked by elaborate ceremonies, an ecstatic "emergence" from the cult house after many months of seclusion, a symbolized "death," a period of inner clarification and the taking on of a new name, cicatrizations, "resurrection" from the physical stress that goes with a cataleptic condition, with the rituals prolonged through days of elaborate dancing performances. The novitiates then returned to their homes where they advanced to a more elevated status. Men and women passed through variegated careers, underwent dietary regimes and periods of continence. Around this nucleus of devotees thousands of believers accepted a life of discipline involving sacrifices of animals, food, and money, and continued services under the control of the priestly hierarchy to one of the many gods to whose circle the officiating priest personally belonged.

THE ECONOMIC BALANCE OF RELIGION

To the student of Dahomean society the drawing of a balance from the economic angle is indicated at this point. The question is how to evaluate the socioeconomic contribution of the sib compound and of ancestor worship respectively to the rural economy of Dahomey.

We dispose only of vague figures in regard to the part of the population that was engaged on a nationwide scale—as priests, diviners, and novitiates—in the worship of the great gods. Burton thought a quarter of the female population was thus withdrawn from their compound and maintained by it. Another source estimated those not drawn into instituted worship totaled less than half the population. Established cult houses were associated with all sib collectivities and modest shrines existed in every compound. The great material burden thrown on the sibs by way of maintenance of the personnel of the cult house was even surpassed by that of sacrifices, fees, gifts, and cooked meals offered to the gods by the sibs several times in the week. Descriptions of Dahomean life put the amount thus diverted from human consumption at an enormous sum. Herskovits stressed that the "conspicuous consumption" thus displayed by the sib was to his mind the chief motivation behind what he regarded as the wealth-getting activities and the gainful businesses transacted by the Dahomean middle classes.

We might be tempted to gauge how much of the annual crops and, even more importantly, what portion of the revenue derived from the entailed palm-oil trees was devoted to religious consumption. Indeed, but for the massive fraction of trustee property that was protected through entail from being spent, the compounds may well have been ruined by the costs of the cult. Short of clear evidence of invested wealth it appears doubtful whether the preconquest sib was in business at all. The twentieth century may have brought about a certain move from religious expenditure to commercial investment. For the eighteenth and nineteenth centuries, however, the weight of the evidence speaks for a religious excoriation of the economy, which scarcely would leave a margin for commercial enterprise. The landed estates of high officials, unless definitely used as plantations and exploited for wholesale marketing, can scarcely serve as proof of a considerable free income seeing the almost unlimited commitments for the servicing of the cult. Prerevolutionary Mexico, Hungary, or Tibet may have had economies burdened to a comparable extent by overgrown establishments and family habits of worship, but then their churches were endowed with riches and owned vast landed possessions. The Dahomean sib compound was decapitalized by a permanent ecclesiastical draining.

CHAPTER SIX

Exchange: Isolated Markets

The preceding chapters have shown how the economic process was embedded in the main institutions of Dahomean society. It was traceable in the palace and the Annual Customs of the state sphere, and in the voluntary work teams and mutual aid associations, as well as in the sib compound and its ancestor worship in the nonstate sphere.

NO PRICE-MAKING MARKETS

Dahomey's markets did not function as price-making markets. They retailed food (much of it cooked), at set prices and, to some extent, the products of handicrafts. The market was strictly monetized: the use of money was compulsory. No barter was permitted. Goods had to be sold for money, and money was used for purchase. Purchases were for cash. There was neither credit nor wholesaling, but the seller was assured of a reasonably stable reward at the set price. This was provided in various ways by producers' organizations which occasionally changed the set rate. Price differentials between local markets caused no movements of goods between the markets; thus no credits or debts existed which might be carried into another market, and no profits were realized through speculation between different markets. Hence nothing in the way of a market system could emerge.

Indeed, the vital function of the market in distributing cooked food proved its propinquity to householding, that ancient form of economic integration in a peasant society. Householding and the market may be thought of here as alternative ways of organizing the distribution of food, the one or the other being made use of as circumstances permit. The king's guests at the capital were provisioned daily by the women of the royal house who carried cooked food from one establishment to another. A similar practice obtained in Whydah kingdom before its conquest, the King of Whydah daily supplying the tables of some 4,000 retainers (Burton, 1893[II]:43), as well as the establishments of the resident European governors. The guests of the Dahomean monarch, in traveling back and forth to Abomey or further inland, were provided for at the "King's Houses"—special stations in towns en route staffed by resident officials or by women of the royal household—or by local chiefs at the king's order. Alternatively, where such facilities were not at hand, travelers lived off the roadside or village markets. Every visitor to Abomey, on his departure from the capital, was to this end "passed" with cowries to defray the expenses of his party on the journey (cf. Dalzel, 1793:146 and Burton, 1893[II]:178, n.1).

Provisioning from household stores thus had narrow geographical limits. Certain semipublic officials were supported partly by rationing and partly through the market. The "public prostitutes" in Abomey mentioned by Norris (in Dalzel, 1793), Burton (1893), and others, seem to have been provided for as members of the royal household in addition to receiving a fixed fee for their services, while those who were stationed in villages throughout the kingdom supplemented their fees by preparing foodstuffs, beer, etc., to sell in the market.

Internal mobility was certainly helped by the market. Traders and other travelers in the interior of the country had recourse to the roadside markets, while the town markets—at least those of Whydah and other seaside towns, though perhaps not in the interior—furnished the daily bread for hired workers. Carriers, hammock men, canoe men, etc., many of whom were aliens and not attached to resident households, received wages called "subsistence," in cowries, with which they purchased food in the market. Burton remarks that "many a 'working man' breakfasts and dines in the alley"

(1893[I]:48), the "alley" being his term for the Zobeme Market at Whydah.

Duncan's description (1847[I]:289) is, as usual, detailed and realistic. Markets along the road, where the traveler might stop for refreshment, chiefly consisted of provisions and articles necessary on the journey such as *kankie,* the native bread made of corn and palm oil, roast beef, and elephant's flesh, as well as boiled pork and goat's flesh. Ready-cooked yams, manioc, and sometimes sweet potatoes were also sold. Water, as well as the native drink, *peto,* was sold at a high price. On the famed road between Kana and Abomey, a royal showpiece, there was a roadside market, mentioned by Skertchly, where the traveler could stop for refreshment (1874:153). These markets along the road also served as local food markets, as did the casual "bush markets."

The bush markets supplied the village or township through the intermediary of the vendors, who were the women of the neighborhood. In these retail markets, prices were set and no institutionalized expression was given to changing forces of supply and demand.

The set price market may offer paradoxical features to the European observer who is used to linking excitement in the market with the ever-contentious matter of prices. Burton's comment might be quoted:

It is a curious contrast, the placidity and impassiveness with which the seller, hardly taking the trouble to remove her pipe, drawls out the price of her two-cowrie lots, and the noisy excitement of the buyers, who know that they must purchase and pay the demand. (1893[I]:49)

As Skertchly remarks, higgling and haggling was of no avail to the buyer. "Notwithstanding the noisy excitement among the buyers, the price of the articles is seldom abated a single cowrie" (1874:28). The solution to the puzzle is that the excited higgling would not have the price for its object, but one or another of the following aspects of the transaction: first, whether the wares for sale qualified for the set price; second, whether the measures handled by the vendor were fair; third, whether the proportions in which the price was supposed to be

paid in the different currencies were just. Also, the picture is
apt to change suddenly if the vendors feel compelled to stand
up for their rights. Herskovits puts stories on record of how the
market women

protect themselves against individuals who come to the market, take
goods, and refuse to pay the standard prices by administering a sound
beating to an offender, with all the aroused women of the group partici-
pating. (1938[I]:61)

COMPULSORY USE OF MONEY

The set price was inseparably linked with that other feature
of the Dahomean markets, the compulsory monetization of sale-
purchase. As early as 1694 Captain Phillips reported on the use
of cowrie as money in Whydah, that "without these shells they
can purchase nothing" (1746:244). From the coast to the
Middle Niger this surprising feature of the market widely
prevailed, a surprising fact, since most of these economies were
"in kind," including the elaborate staple finances of the
governmental center itself. Yet Binger noted for the Western
Sudan in the late nineteenth century,

In general in these countries direct exchange does not exist; before making
a purchase you must convert your goods into the currency of the country.
(1892[I]:2)

Or Basden, speaking about the contemporary markets of the
Ibo,

All goods are sold in the terms of the local currency; there is no bartering
of commodities in exchange for other commodities. (1921:196–97)

Skertchly, writing about the above-mentioned snack bar adjoining the gala road between Kana and Abomey, offers idio-
matic evidence of how strongly that trait was ingrained. His
bush market carries in its name the facetious warning "cash
only." It is called

Akwe-janahan. Akwe, cowries—*janahan*, suppose you have none—meaning
that "here is the market, but if you have not brought any cowries it is
of no use to you." (1874:153)

Short of the monetization of the isolated markets, set food prices would not have been practicable. As we shall later see, the most striking achievement of the Dahomean statesmanship, the stable rate of exchange of cowrie and gold, rested on set prices for food in that microcosm, the local market.

NO CREDIT, CASH ONLY

Another localizing feature was the prevention of the development of credit that would have passed on the effects of transactions from one market to another market of the "ring." Phillips identified the general use of cowrie in the market with cash payments, and Labat confirms in 1727 that in Whydah "No credit is known in this country. . . . One pays up before receiving the merchandise" (Labat, 1731[II]:166), though he specifies that both gold dust and cowrie are current. Basden in our own times stresses of the Ibo that in their markets "each transaction is an entirely separate and distinct affair" (1921:197). Analytically, this is conclusive evidence of the absence of a market system.

RETAILER'S REWARD: DOUBLE NUMERATION

In these isolated markets, the Dahomean woman could count on a stable if limited income earned by her own exertions. This gave her a status in the hierarchy of the organization which regulated and disciplined activities in the province of the market. Much of the day was taken up by trekking, sometimes even twice a day, to the plantations where produce was bought and carried to the market. The preparation of *kankie* bread, *peto* drinks, cooked meats, and pastries that made up the snacks and meals by which they catered to the needs of the male working population kept them so busy as to invite highly appreciative comments of all foreign observers. All this was institutionalized in the isolated food markets that had become the locus of the productive activities of all the women.

Financially the profit margin that served as the vendor's reward had for its source the retailer's discount which again had possible origins of a very different character. Herskovits refers to the wholesaler's allowing for a twenty per cent discount in setting the price of their produce to the retailer, having first ascertained the actual price which the retailed article fetched in the market of the city.

Prices are not fixed by agreement between the *gletanu,* but rather by means of a careful watch kept on the retail market by each man individually. Agents are sent incognito to Abomey to buy grain in the open market, and if, for example, a wholesaler's agent were to buy a measure of meal for one franc, the price to the market women would be set at eighty centimes. (1938[I]:56)

Briefly, there is in operation a regulated equivalency of twenty per cent for the market woman's labor, the method of which is adjustable to circumstances.

According to numerous sources in widely different regions of the Western Sudan, a dual numeration of cowrie money was in use which automatically secured a similar profit to the retailer. Mage wrote in 1868:

les cauris ont une numération toute spéciale. On les compte, par 10, et il semble tout d'abord que le système de numération soit décimal; mais on compte 8 fois 10 = 100; 10 fois 100 = 1000, 10 fois 1000 = 10,000; 8 fois 10,000 = 100,000; ce qui fait que 100,000 . . . n'est en réalité que 64,000, que 10,000 . . . n'est que 8000; que 1000 . . . n'est que 800 et que le 100 n'est que 80 . . . (1868:191)

In 1899, Baillaud gives a similar account:

les cauris se comptent suivant la méthode Bambara, dans laquelle les unités du troisième ordre commencent à 80. Donc, lorsque nous disons que l'on a 5000 cauris pour 5 francs, il faut comprendre 50 fois 80, soit, dans notre numération, 4000! Toutes les fois qu'il s'est agi de cauris, notre administration a été obligée, d'employer cette méthode Bambara, ce qui n'a du reste pas grand inconvénient, lorsqu'on est prévenu. (1902:71)

Baillaud adds the comment: "On concoit que cette difference de cours favorisé le commerce de detail" (*ibid.*:71). That is, retailers who purchased a large quantity of a good valued for example at 10,000 cowries, would actually pay 8,000 cowries for it (cf. also Lenz, 1884[II]:158–59). Yet selling in small retail quantities, where this double numeration did not hold, the vendor would receive full payment of 10,000 cowries and thus make a profit of twenty per cent owing to the monetary system.

While no direct evidence exists for this double numeration of cowrie within Dahomey itself, the persistence in modern times of a procedure regulating profit at twenty per cent suggests an institutional method of profit regulation organized through the currency in historic Dahomey.

SETTING THE PRICES

These markets, as we know, were not price making, i.e., the prices did not fluctuate according to supply and demand. But how were the prices actually set? This was part of the function of producers' organizations, including the bodies consisting of women selling the foodstuffs in that market. As to craft goods, bodies of guilds regulated the conditions of work in their crafts, set standards for the product, maintained discipline, and set the prices for products sold in the market and the retailing procedures.

First, the food prices were by far the predominant item in the market. In the market at Abomey the price was set by the woman who first arrived at the market, and this price was adhered to during the day. In the coastal cities of Whydah and Porto Novo the vendors of the same commodity belonged to societies called *sodudo* which fixed the prices at which foodstuffs were to be sold. "Prices," Herskovits notes, "are set by these societies and each member observes them" (1938[I] :61). When he inquired about price cutting, the women expressed surprise that this should be attempted. It would only reduce profits, and supplies were generally sold by the end of the day anyway.

The *sodudo* also had mutual aid and pseudo-familial functions which bound their members closely together. The illness of a member was the occasion for all to visit and bring gifts. At a member's death all vendors of the same product would absent themselves from the market for eight days during the funeral rites.

The women sellers of foodstuffs in the larger markets pro-

cured their supplies from the specialized farms. Every digni-
tary in Dahomey had a number of plantations and later
qualified for a *gletanu,* that is, a wholesaler (*ibid.*[I]:55).
Some of their farms comprised areas of from fifteen to twenty-
five or thirty kilometers in length and several kilometers in
breadth. They specialized in raising a single food staple such as
millet, maize, or yams. Our information is less complete for the
small markets, but it would seem that the women relied on the
surpluses from their or their husbands' village plots or from the
fields of the compound. The tenacity of the methods of setting
the retail equivalents for produce of the soil, even in modern
times, is striking. When Herskovits made his survey, the retail
price of palm oil was set by the women sellers. The oil was
dispensed in standard containers, and the price varied with the
price of a basket of palm nuts which was in turn determined by
royal decision according to the world market for palm kernels.
To this latter price was added an equivalent for the labor
expended by specialists who prepared and sold the oil.

Secondly, prices were set for craft products. As individual
and nonstandard products, the setting of prices for crafts
differed from that of foodstuffs. But the influence of the craft
guild, or *so,* was dominant throughout the production and sale
of these products.

The weavers were members of certain families which made
up the craft guild and acted in turn as brokers. The looms were
in separate shelters near the compounds where they lived.*
The chief of the principal group of weavers exercised control
over all weavers. Cooperative work was the rule, and weavers
were subject to strict discipline. When a weaver invented a new
pattern, he sent samples to his fellow craftsmen. Each pattern
had a name and prices were fixed according to the design. Since
these were well known, there was little haggling in the market.
The weaver fixed his price by taking the price of native-spun
cotton as a base. Herskovits says that formerly, before cotton
was grown, native raffia was used in this calculation. To the

* Herskovits mentions that to his knowledge there were only three groups of
weavers, all resident in Abomy. (1938[I]:76)

price of cotton, which was ten centimes for a carded piece of forty-two lengths, the weaver added fifteen francs for a woman's cloth or thirty francs for a man's cloth. Thus, if the price of the raw material was fixed, the standard markup would result in a price varying only with the amount of material used in making the piece (Herskovits, 1938[I]:62). Competition in selling was further restricted by limitations on the use of patterns. Any member of the guild had to have the permission of the guild head to sell his cloth or reproduce a design not invented by himself and had to pay for the use of such a design (*ibid.*:76).

Production, as we have said, was governed by a rotation system. The members of a group worked on the material supplied by each member in turn, so that each weaver in succession became the owner of a supply of cloth. A member of a company of weavers was in turn entrusted with the sale of cloth for the account of all the members of his group. He was obliged to render an accounting to the owner of each piece of cloth when the market was over. On default, sanctions were imposed. Herskovits says

... in the instance of a weaver who had given yarn to one of his associates, and this associate had sold the cloth and profited, but when the time came to reciprocate had not given what was expected of him, the *soga* would take action. This would consist of seizing the property of the defaulter, including any of his animals that might be attached and sold. If the culprit had nothing to attach, he would be deprived of his membership in the society, and a complaint would be lodged against him with authorities; in the olden days, it would have been a matter to be taken before the King. (*Ibid.*:254)

Ironworkers likewise were members of given families, worked in rotation, and lived in separate quarters around the forge. Members of a forge worked in common, each smith in turn providing the raw material on which he and his associates worked. The finished product belonged to the one who supplied the materials. There was no fixed price for iron products, each smith selling at his own price, which might be higher or lower depending on his need for cash. Skertchly notes that prices of iron products were determined separately for each object (q. Herskovits, 1938[I]:62, n.1).

The absence of a fixed price was also true of "goldsmiths" working in brass and silver and those who did applique work in cloth. They were regarded as artists rather than as craftsmen and were relatively few in number. For woodcarvings it was expected that a purchaser would continue to pay a woodcarver the same price for pieces of the same relative size in subsequent purchases as he had paid for the first piece (*ibid.*:62).

While men carried on the work in iron and in cloth; pottery, the third principal craft, was in the hands of women. Groups of women used a kiln in common, making their pottery individually or with a few helpers but firing it cooperatively. The sellers of pottery waited until all the pottery of a given type had come into the marketplace before setting the price for the day (*ibid.*:61). Of the makers of pots, Herskovits writes,

A woman who does not get on with the others of her group, particularly if she cuts her prices, is punished not only by having her stock of pottery broken by her associates, but also by being forced to work for a time without remuneration before she is readmitted to all the privileges of the guild. (*Ibid.*:76–77)

CHANGING THE SET PRICE

How did the set prices change? In general, prices were changed in the same way in which they were originally set, but the system had an inelasticity of its own. A change of prices did not necessarily bring about a corresponding change in "supply." Even a seasonally high price did not induce competition among sellers. Also, the state maintained, as we saw, overall supervision of agriculture through the *Tokpo* and his officials. Annual inspection of the crops took place, permitting changes in the production of various crops to be commanded. Changes in "supply" did not as a rule result from local price changes but rather from administrative decisions. Herskovits writes:

When there was an overproduction of one crop and an underproduction of another, the crop of an entire district might be changed at his [the *Tokpo's*] command. (*Ibid.*:112)

Forbes described a discussion of the agricultural situation by the king and his ministers at a state session during the period of the Annual Customs, but it would seem that the central authority may have confined itself to regulating the supply of foodstuffs, leaving matters of price to local bodies which were, however, most reluctant to interfere with traditional food prices. Add to this the general absence of price differentials over extended regions and we will understand why no trade based on market functions is encountered. To this fact we shall return.

CHEAP FOOD

These unimpressive market institutions functioned in a fairly effective way. The universal cheapness of the means of subsistence that resulted impressed itself upon all European observers. This is particularly true of Whydah, whether still subject to Ardra, already independent, or, eventually, under Dahomean rule. It contrasted on ecological grounds with Whydah's immediate neighbors to the west, the bleak areas of the lagoon-dwelling Popos, a region of semi-starvation mitigated only by the catch from the sea and lagoon. The bounty of nature did not, of course, favor inland Dahomey as it did the gardenlike strip of Whydah. Nevertheless, our authors, visiting Dahomey and referring to its economic condition, scarcely ever remarked on any stringency of livelihood or shortages of food. No paupers or beggars were in evidence. With the returning skippers the supplying of their live cargo with food was of course a standing concern. The native chiefs often withheld access to inland food markets, wishing to exert pressure on business lines, but no complaints of the price of foodstuffs being raised are in evidence. Native tactics merely aimed at evoking delays which threatened the skipper with ruinous losses. At no time was it the price of the food supplies that caused the squeeze.

The absence of native records in the nonliterate coastal areas, as well as inland Dahomey, leaves the economic historian of the eighteenth century with scant data to substantiate assertions on the extraordinary cheapness of living. Yet the period of over a hundred and fifty years separating Barbot and Bosman from Duncan, Forbes, Burton, and Skertchly offers a factually well-supported picture of a simple material culture nowise lacking in ease of life in regard to nutrition.

For the stability of the currency there is good evidence. It suffices to refer to the rate of 32,000 cowries to the ounce gold, equaling 4 pounds sterling, which was at no time in doubt over that period. This fact alone permits us to evoke the unanimous expressions of surprise over the cheapness of life in that vast area extending north to south from Libya to the Guinea Coast, and west to east from the neighborhood of the Atlantic to Lake Tchad by eminent scholars of Germany, France, and England. They insisted that the necessaries of life could be bought for a very few cowries, supported by a precise reference to the metallic exchange value of the cowrie.

Nachtigal elaborated on the democratic effects of cowrie. A cowrie, he said, represented "a Thaler split into 4000 shells . . . which enables the poor to buy the most minute quantity of any divisible object or material" (1879[I]:692). Heinrich Barth, who was present before cowrie made its appearance in the Central Sudan, wrote

The fatigue which people have to undergo in purchasing their week's necessaries in the market is all the more harassing as there is not at present any standard money for buying and selling. (1859)

He was skeptical at first of the public policy which introduced cowries "rather by a speculation of the ruling people than by a natural want of the inhabitants" (*ibid.*), as he suspected. The *gabagas* or native cotton strips of fourteen yards length had deteriorated into rags. The exchange value of the new currency was fixed as low as eight cowries equal to a cotton strip. Barth eventually agreed that the shells "are very useful for buying small articles and infinitely more convenient than the cotton strips" (*ibid.*). Nachtigal highly approved of the ubiquitous cowrie, the value of which he calculated at about one tenth of a *pfennig* (1879[I]:692). Its comparable English gold value was almost exactly one eighth of a farthing. Simone Berbain, the French authority, puts the value of one cowrie in French terms at one fifth of a *liard* (1942:69), i.e., of half a farthing. The advantages of the minute monetary unit may have been obscured during a brief inflationary period of the cowrie currency. Burton and Skertchly witnessed such a rise in prices in Whydah, when the *kankie* rose from three to twelve cowries. But Skertchly, though listing the price rises, added the remark that nonetheless "in every shop there are to be seen plenty of two-cowrie lots" (1874:28). For on the stalls there would be displayed the usual couple of sewing needles, safety pins, a dozen corns of pepper, a pinch of salt, an arm's length of white cotton thread, a thimble of refreshing beverage, a mouthful of mutton or goat's meat, well done and seasoned. Almost two centuries before—about 1694—Commander Thomas Phillips of the *Hannibal,* of London, visiting the seat of the King of Whydah, took time off to remark on a shady cluster of trees where a small market was kept.

Among other things in it I observed an ordinary, which, for the novelty of it I shall describe: It was kept at the foot of one of the largest trees; the master thereof had for a table a plate of flat wood, about a yard diameter, which was placed on the ground. The meat was beef and dog's flesh boiled, wrap'd up in a raw cow's hide, and placed on one side, and an earthen crock with boiled cancies in it to serve for bread on the other.

An informal meal followed, though in style:

When any one came to eat he would down on his knees by the table, and lay eight or nine cowrie shells thereon; then the cook would very dexterously cut him the value of what he pitched on in small bits, and give him his piece of cancy and some salt; if that did not satisfy his stomach, he would lay down more shells, and accordingly have more meat.

Cowrie was up to the performance:

I have seen eight or nine round his table at once, and he served them all, and received their money with great dexterity, and without the least confusion; but there was no need to change money, which was a great ease to him. (1746:238–39)

SEPARATENESS OF EXTERNAL TRADE
FROM THE MARKET

The reluctance of supply to respond to rising food prices in isolated markets has already been remarked upon. Students of the ancient economy will be reminded of the fact that in early society, whether primitive or archaic, external trade and local markets do not show the close connectedness to which we are accustomed in our modern society. The ubiquitous markets of Dahomey do not in this regard behave in the modern way for the simple reason that only market *systems* with their price differentials direct the course of trade.

Since Dahomey's economy is signally lacking in that elaboration of the exchange pattern which is the market system, we should expect a great dearth of any other than the administered forms of governmental trading, operated from the center, serving army and foreign trade. No private merchants, only swarms of dependent porters and distinguished officials briefed as military guards and commercial diplomats form the personnel of the typical caravan. The figure of the middle-class merchant, such as the Islamic trading mullah, is a transient in Dahomey. Its countryside knows no middle-distance trading; closer to the border towns where the newly acquired, non-incorporated areas of Dahomey lay and where there was still room for private caravan trading, the existence of outer and inner markets of the towns demonstrated the distinction of trade and market. The oncoming trader was met by the caboceer in the outer market where the caboceer acquired wholesale the goods which it was his privilege to have retailed for profit by his wives within the town and partly to have peddled by adolescents in the huts of the neighboring villages. In Duncan's vivid words:

The old man [caboceer of Baffo] seemed all in a bustle, this being the principal market-day in Baffo; and he is allowed still to maintain an ancient custom, which existed here previous to the subjection of the Mahee country, of monopolizing the whole trade of the place to himself. In consequence of this, he was busily employed in watching his young

wives who kept stalls, or hawked their goods in the market place, many
of whom I believe possessed very little personal interest in their divided
spouse's profits, but in order to render theft impracticable, he placed all
his youngest wives in the most conspicuous parts of the marketplace and
himself occupied a position which commanded a view of the whole scene.
The older or more trustworthy wives were permitted to use their own discretion as to their choice of carrying their goods round the different parts
of the town. The principal or favourite wives dole out the portions of goods
allotted to each individual to sell, but it often occurs that they are sold
at even a higher price than designed by the owner, particularly when
strangers are the purchasers. Of course the extra charge is appropriated
by the individual seller. (1847[II]:47–8)

Part II has dealt with the economy of the inland kingdom
of Dahomey which after 1727 administered also the Port of
Trade of Whydah on the Guinea Coast. Up to the middle of the
nineteenth century, Abomey was the capital of a flourishing
archaic empire. In the main, the four integrative patterns—
redistribution, reciprocity, householding, and market exchange
—seem to have accounted for the functioning of the economy.
In the absence of statistical data we are reduced to gauging
success and failure by the economic historian's customary
markers of social welfare or its opposite. Social equilibrium, a
stable standard of life or, alternatively, famine, depopulation,
and civil commotion are such indicators. A vital seismograph of
monetized economies is the degree of the stability of the currency. Though only partially monetized, Dahomey's massive
foreign trade exposed its exchanges to an unusually strenuous
test. But how, without an equilibrating mechanism as represented by the market system, could stable exchanges be maintained in peace and war over more than a century? The rigid
structural solidity of the archaic economy must appear at this
stage of our analysis as the alternative to equilibrating devices.

PART III

The Slave Trade

CHAPTER SEVEN

Whydah: Institutional Origins of a Port of Trade

PORTS OF TRADE IN EARLY SOCIETIES

The port of trade was an institution comparable in function and efficiency to our international marketplaces, while restricted to operational methods foreign to the competitive supply-demand-price mechanism with which we are familiar (Polanyi, 1963). The origins of the port of trade as an institution reach far back in history. Its rationale was to offer to the trader safety of life and limb as well as of property. The meeting of strangers on foreign coasts accompanied all early trade, and so did the hazards inseparable from these meetings. Hence the ancient practice of dumb barter or silent trade on deserted beaches, as Herodotus described the Phoenicians, bartering salt for gold on the northern Guinea Coast, two thousand years before our period.

In the emergence of ports of trade in civilized areas, three features generally were present: economic administration, political neutrality, and ease of transportation. Trade was transacted not through price competition but my means of administrative acts; the port authorities were committed to political nonalignment; finally, neutral waterways, whether coastal, paludal, or riverine, were essential for cheap carrying.

Safety depended on island sites, systems of waterways, marshes and lagoons, peninsular location, a mountain fastness such as Petra, desert environments, or a combination of these. Each of them offered a variety of tactical advantages in Mediterranean, Asian, African, and Central American subcontinents. Ugarit, El Mina, Tyre, Syracuse, Miletus, Naukratis,

99

the Piraeus, Rhodes, Carthage, Corinth, Alexandria are insular or peninsular examples; Tmutorokan, Karakorum, Kandahar, and Timbuktu were circled by desert tracts; and some island centers were Goree, James Fernando Po, Prince's Island off the West African coast, Xoconusco, Xicolango in Mexico, and the Malabars.

As a rule the port of trade was situated in militarily "weak hands" such as tribal communities or small kingdoms, so that the disembarking foreigner need not fear being robbed of his wares, dragged into slavery, or killed outright. Only at the extreme counterpole of weak hands, namely, under strong, ordered government did the trader meet again with reassuring conditions. Unless the government was both capable and willing to defend its neutrality and to enforce law and impartial justice, foreign merchants had to avoid places occupied by military power.

A case in point was Cortez' visit in force to Acalan, a riverine town situated in an area between the Mexican and the Mayan empires. Acalan, a town harboring hundreds of pirogues, originally was no more than a tribal area, famous as a center where riverine and paludal traders met with the men of the hills. Cortez, marching into Acalan only a few years later as a conqueror, was surprised to find that it had ceased to be a trading place. Actually, the change was caused by its having been incorporated into a military empire, his own. Its neutrality was now jeopardized and its attraction had ceased for the tribes which used to frequent it with the produce of the forests of the distant mountains.

Another instance antedates sixteenth-century Mexico by more than a millenium. The resplendent caravan city of Palmyra in Roman Syria has been characterized by Rostovtzeff as having been in the nature of a port of trade where Parthian and Roman traders belonging to enemy countries met, trekking through the desert from east to west and from west to east. Hence, he argued, the refusal of the Romans to garrison Palmyra. Rather, they fell back and restricted themselves to a kind of remote control of that caravan city. The army was deliberately kept at a distance to reassure the Arabs emerging from the desert that no danger was attached to their entering the neighborhood of the city, which was artificially endowed with a sort of international neutrality highly advantageous to its commercial prosperity. Rostovtzeff assumed that even written agreements between Parthians and Romans may have been concluded (1932:103). Yet another historical case is that of Whydah itself, which flourished as a neutral port, safeguarded by treaty. Its conquest by the Dahomean empire caused for a time a decline of the slave trade, the small suppliers now keeping aloof.

The student of economic development then may ask: How, about the turn of the seventeenth century A.D., did the obscure coastal strip of Upper Guinea inhabited by the Houeda tribe of the lagoons establish itself as an independent administration, make itself felt as a center of the world slave trade, and within a year or two formally declare itself a neutral in the great wars that were raging between the powers of the age? The answer must be sought in the military, technical, and economic needs of the Afro-American slave trade which struck precisely at that time and in that spot of the West African coast.

Three regions of the African coast should be distinguished in regard to the historical evolution of the slave trade. The first was the Gold Coast on which, besides gold, slaves were bought even before the onrush of the Afro-American slave trade which reached the Gold Coast in the 1660's. Then, moving eastward and inland from the coast, we come to the Kingdom of Ardra during the quarter century of transition from gold trade to slave trade, 1669–1704. The third region was the small kingdom of Whydah, formerly a tributary of Ardra, borne to statehood by the tidal wave of the slave trade toward the very end of the seventeenth century. Its independent port of trade arose as the loose archaic empire structure of Ardra proved unequal to the requirements of the "modern" slave trade (1704–27).

In each of these regions and periods, the manner in which trade was transacted depended upon the political organization of the coastal area and its hinterland. This influenced decisively the institutional channels by which the "goods" were forthcoming, as well as their ordered disposal, or the play of "supply" and "demand" as the economist would prefer to call it. In the absence of a market mechanism the economic process was here channeled through the intermediacy of the political organization which took on unusual forms.

SLAVE TRADE ON THE GOLD COAST

The Gold Coast was no more than a narrow strip between the beach and the range of thickly wooded mountains washed by tropical rains. It was mostly a sandy waste, a scraggy bush stretching right to the River Volta where the river-gold on coast and hinterland abruptly ended. Small, sparsely inhabited fishing villages parts of tribal communities, dotted the coast; none of them presenting itself as an organized state. The gold trade was carried on by the simple means of Europeans bartering their miscellaneous wares for gold, either as Castle trade, i.e., from warehouses (factories), or from their ships. "Castle trade" sounds more imposing than were the modest stores staffed by a few employees, mostly natives, with only a few substantial fortifications—El Mina and Capo Corso—designed as a protection for the factories, mainly against European competitors. Most of the trade was carried on as "ship trade," particularly where slaves were concerned. Native brokers, mostly by night, rowed out to passing skippers with one or two or at most three slaves. Not even the gold trade was transacted between the European countries and native collectivities in set forms, in the absence of native political units required for commercial relations between strangers on foreign coasts.

Bosman's (1814) incisive distinction between monarchies and republics on the Guinea Coast is the key to the political organization of the area—his eloquent praise of the orderly realms of the absolute despots, as he calls them, mainly in the interior, and his discounting of the tribal republics and their unstable federations stringing along the coast as weak and ineffectual. The Corn, Tooth, and Gold coasts of Guinea pos-

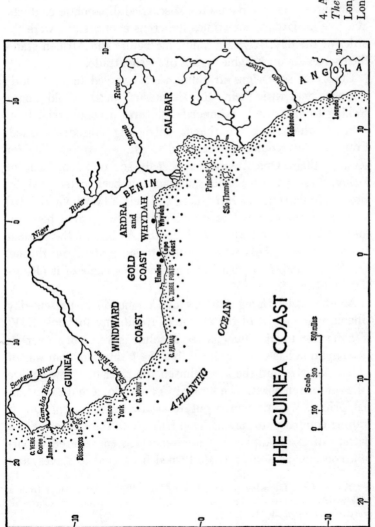

THE GUINEA COAST

Scale
0   100   300   500 miles

4. Adapted from K. G. Davies,
The Royal African Company,
Longmans, Green and Co.
London, 1957.

sessed scarcely any organized states on the beaches, in contrast to the small bureaucratic monarchies of Whydah and Porto Novo of the Slave Coast proper.

Contemporary European powers of the middle seventeenth century were slow to understand the implications of these conditions for trade.* In effect, the European-chartered companies had no native partners to treat with, nor consequently trade agreements to live up to. Miscarried diplomatic contacts, abortive initiatives, sometimes ludicrous contretemps were the order of the day. It was a long time before the African states themselves set up suitable organs of foreign trade.

European sovereigns at times were engaged in diplomatic arrangements with their "Royal cousins" of the Gold Coast, seeking to gain through honorific gestures a commercial foothold on the Black Continent. Intriguing episodes ensued. France, a latercomer on the Gold Coast, was responsible for some of them. One Aniaba, supposedly son of Zena, King of Issiny, was sent to France and, having been catechized by Bossuet in person, was introduced to Louis XIV who appointed him an officer of the Horse and eventually became his godfather. After his return to Issiny—the Assinie of the present Ivory Coast—Aniaba was expected to succeed to the throne. But he was shown up as a fraud and nothing came of it (Roussier, 1935:xvii ff.).

Another ruler, King Amoysy of Commendo in present-day Ghana, made a gift of the village of Aquitagny to Louis XIV, transferring to him by charter absolute sovereignty over it. Investigation has since revealed that the Issiny kingdom was of Lilliputian size and the king himself the ruler of a few square miles of barren coast. The king of Commendo, a more substantial prince, was promptly put to death by the local Dutch trading company for having been friendly to the French. Yet a pattern of exotic diplomacy was set which engendered important consequences when trade turned from gold to slaves, and

---

* This and the following paragraph have been distilled by Polanyi from a wide variety of sources; it has not been possible to reconstruct the sources of every factual statement [Ed.].

that on an enormously enhanced scale. The native ruler might now tend to regard foreign diplomatic contacts as a substitute for a commercial bureaucracy of his own, capable of providing the intricate and costly administration required for the whole-sale exporting of slaves. The pattern of commercial arrange-ment favored by the native chiefdoms—not necessarily also by regular monarchies—was to invest the European sovereign with the monopoly of the slave trade in his country on the understanding that the European partner undertake the organ-izing of this complex and risky business.

The change from gold to slaves happened rather abruptly about 1670 at the eastern end of the Gold Coast, beyond the River Volta, and in the somewhat vaguely defined kingdom of Ardra. Within a generation—by 1704—it was to raise to world prominence the kingdom of Whydah, a small coastal tributary of Ardra. An unprecedented supply of slaves had made its appearance in Ardra, and this situation demanded more ade-quate institutional methods to deal by than Ardra could provide. To understand the actual forces at work in this trans-formation, the requirements of this peculiar trade under the given conditions must be considered.

About 1675 a falling-off of trade on the Gold Coast was noted. Skippers were induced to drift further east after gold but without success. Simultaneously, in the West Indies the demand for slaves was rising sharply. Accordingly, the Sgr. D'Amon who in the 1670's had been busily pursuing dramatic French diplomacy in Issiny in a futile attempt to further the gold trade returned to Issiny by the end of the century, this time to persuade the king to change over from gold to slaves, but in vain, for the slave caravans hit the coast farther east. From far inland, from the north, thousands of slaves were already on the move along the Gap of Benin, headed for Ardra and Whydah. The historic slave rush was on.

ARDRA: TRANSITION

West African slave trade, which started in the mid-seven-teenth century as "single trade" on the Gold Coast, reached its spectacular height in the late seventeenth century in Whydah on the Slave Coast. Between these two stretches of time and location there was a short but significant period of transition— in Ardra from 1670 to 1704. From scant historical evidence we may nevertheless follow the antecedents of the port of trade from its incubation in Ardra as it evolved through the strains and stresses of the last two decades of the seventeenth century into a full-fledged institution of world trade in Whydah.

Only twice before had recorded history touched upon the African inland state of Ardra: first in 1671, with Carolof of the French West Indies Company; next in 1704, with Jean Doublet (called the Pirate), shareholder of the same company which was now named *de l'Asiente*. In the interim Ardra was acting intermittently as the matrix of that vast movement of trade which was to change the socioeconomy of whole sub-continents in the Western hemisphere. But the time was not yet. The African yield of slaves would have to increase manyfold, speeded by the commercial innovations introduced in Whydah. At Ardra itself growth would be slow. True, the powers were bent on extracting slaves from Africa for use in America at all cost. In the absence of a market system, however, the process had to rely on the existing institutional fixtures, which, in the nature of things, were not commercial at all but rather political.

The growing slave trade was, therefore, embedded over a generation in the territorial bodies that comprised the loosely knit state organization of the kingdom of Ardra and its vassal chiefdoms. Big or small, they derived a money income from taxing the slave trade. Ardra imposed the payment of a con-siderable lump sum, the custom, on every ship for the permis-sion to trade within the empire and set a fixed toll per head on slaves entering its area, as well as an equal toll if they were being sold abroad (Barbot, 1732:349–50). The king was the chief beneficiary of custom and toll, apart from earnings from ancillary commercial services.

The inland center of the empire pressed on with the supply-ing of slaves, while the coastal units were supposed to provide the channels of distribution which served as an outlet for the European demand. However, there was no organ of coordination in this political setting to provide a responsive link between the oncoming slaves and the chances for an outlet, since the central government lacked administrative personnel within the zone of its warlike seafaring tributaries.

The abnormality of it all was that the territory where the inflow of slaves to Ardra from the north met with the agents of the European slavers who represented the outflow in the south was no more than a mere patch of land a good day's journey across to the right and left of the village of Little Ardra. Facing north, this small area was the recipient of slaves originating in a vast reservoir of inland supply; facing south, toward the ocean, it was spurting slaves toward the beaches. It was not identified with any single tribe, city, or small state; apart from Whydah and Porto Novo, it lay amid suborganized territories of unruly tribes, most of whom fought each other. Geographically, it was covered by a maze of slow rivers and extended lagoons separated from the beach and from one another by broad strips of marshland. This was primarily the condition of that part of the coast of which Ardra was the suzerain, with its traditional capital, Alladah, about thirty-five miles from the sea. This was practically the range at which all Guinea state capitals, whether Ashanti, Dahomey, Oyo, Yoruba, or Benin, lay from the ocean. Each country remained at a safe distance from the sea which was taboo to their rulers. None possessed a fleet nor practiced other than river, lake, or lagoon fishing. The notion of shouldering administrative tasks on the coast was utterly foreign to them. Their contact with the sea was limited to suzerainty over fishing tribes largely living a life of their own.

The sprawling empire of Ardra controlled, then, neither the northern supply nor the southern outlet of slaves. The king of Ardra did not purchase slaves for export in the inland markets nor carry on systematic raids across his borders. Caravans from the north were the organs of supply, and the king was scarcely able to stagger the oncoming supply once it had started to flow from its distant sources. No more adequate was the king's control of the outlet. The small fishing states were in a condition of chronic rebellion. There was always the temptation of selling the slaves on their own; admitting the eager European buyers to their local food markets; smuggling slaves through officially closed passes; disrupting Ardra's arrangements with European slavers; dislodging foreign factors, plundering their warehouses if not murdering them outright; sabotaging their factories; subverting the native villages that surrounded the European forts; sharing in the intrigues of the chartered companies and native personalities on which in the last resort the chances of smooth transportation and transactions rested.

To illustrate this pattern of local conflicts and European interventions we have the witness of Barbot (1732) and Bosman (1814). Proceeding east from the Volta we find the Coto, the Little and Great Popos, Whydah, Jaquin, and Offra—or Little Ardra, as it was called by the Europeans. This was the hub of the region whence an excellent road led to Great Ardra or Assem on the River Lagos, the commercial capital of Ardra.

The people of Coto were warring indecisively with the Little Popos, a practice favored by their common hinterland neighbor, the Aquambos. The Little Popos, again, often acted as the strong arm of the king of Ardra. When Offra rebelled against Ardra in the 1670's and the Dutch factor, a favorite of the king, was murdered, the king persuaded the Little Popos to attack the Offra, destroy them, and deliver their chief into his hands. Afterward, Barbot recounted (1732:452) "pushed on by the King of Ardra," the Little Popos "marched against the people of Whydah and encamped in their country. After being repulsed, their chief attacked the Cotos and perished in battle. The present king" says Barbot, "revenged his brother's death on the Cotosians" (*ibid.*), who were eventually driven out of their country. This happened about 1700.

Proceeding to Great Popos, a sequence of foreign interventions is on record. Their king, we are told, gained the throne by replacing his brother with the help of the French, who then made him tributary to Whydah. The Great Popos, however, "threw off their yoke," but were again invaded by the Whydasians assisted by the French fleet. The attackers suffered heavy losses and were quite unable to dislodge the Popos from their island seat in the lagoon (Barbot, 1732:452–53). Bosman (1814), visiting Whydah—at that time another disaffected tributary of Ardra—found the king there very popular with the Europeans. Indeed, he had been elevated to the throne with French and English help, his brother having first been deprived of it. Bosman prophesied another civil war upon the demise of the popular monarch, whose younger son, he thought, was likely to be favored by the Europeans against his elder brother. Soon afterward exactly that came to pass, an event closely associated with the setting up of the port of trade at Whydah.

The impotence of the king of Ardra to deal with the much smaller Whydah, his incapacity to break the even smaller and weaker Popos, and other political paradoxes resulted largely from the tactical advantages of impregnable lagoon positions amid almost impassable marshes and mud lakes. The political organization of the outlet area appears, then, to have been quite inadequate to channel an economic process that assumed some correspondence between resources offered and the chances of their distribution. The situation was, indeed, anomalous. A new movement of trade, spanning the coasts of whole subcontinents—South America and West Africa, reaching in either case far into the respective hinterlands—had been set in motion in almost total absence of a physical and institutional contact between the goods and their potential users.

The kingdom of Ardra on the Guinea Coast was of roughly semicircular shape, arching eastward toward the coast. Its northern limits were supposed to extend into the bush toward Benin (*ibid.*:346), yet its only direct access to the sea at Offra (Little Ardra) was no more than a land channel three quarters of a mile wide. For the rest, Ardra was separated from the ocean by a band of maritime communities (including Whydah and Porto Novo) representing more or less loyal tributaries. As

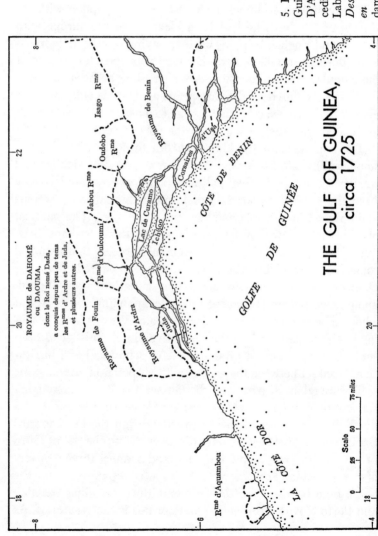

5. Fragment of a map of the Guinea Coast drawn by Sr D'Anville for Volume I (preceding page 1) of Père J. B. Labat, *Voyage Du Chevalièr Des Marchais En Guinée* ... *en 1725, 1726, 1727.* Amsterdam, 1731.

ROYAUME de DAHOMÉ ou DAOUMA, dont le Roi nomé Dada, a conquis depuis peu de tems les R^mes d'Ardre et de Juda, et plusieurs autres.

THE GULF OF GUINEA, circa 1725

an organ of the slave trade, Ardra operated somewhat as a funnel, open to the north, that ended in a damper from which slaves were released in all directions.

The royal government required that slaves be tolled, since taxes levied on trade were the main source of its revenue from the slave trade. The king's interest, therefore, lay in the largest possible number of slaves to pass through his territories so long as none went untolled and the foreign trader who eventually bought the slave had personally paid the customs to him. In what way the slave was sold was otherwise of little concern to the king, so long as the selling "hand" previously presented the slave for tolling to the king's officers at Great Ardra, only two miles from the trade center of Assem. This requirement may have been operationally difficult to meet for some coastal vassals. Great Popo revolted once in protest against Ardrasian constraint that all slaves sold by Poposians must first be taken to Great Ardra for tolling. This, however, was only one of several requirements of the slave trade difficult to square with the political embeddedness of the outlet for the slave trade under Ardrasian aegis. The selection of slaves by the various purchasers, their feeding and guarding, the transporting to and fro, and their branding with regard to different purchasing nations, complicated by unseasonal weather conditions as well as by military considerations, raised intricate problems of administration affecting the profitability of the undertaking. Massive losses could accrue, mainly through delays caused in loading that in turn delayed completion of the return voyage, thus increasing the average costs to the slavers.

The lack of synchronization between the European purchasers and the native suppliers of the trade was present from the beginning. The European's promise to send merchandise remained sometimes unfulfilled for years. However, while the gold waiting for him on the Gold Coast did not have to be subsisted and guarded in crowded barracoons, undelivered slaves were a heavy burden in the absence of the expected customers. In the first decade of the slave rush Ardra suffered from gluts of slaves owing to the grand gestures of French governments which eventually failed to live up to their commitments of shipping any number of slaves as soon as they were available (D'Elbée, 1671 [II]:407). At times the position was reversed, and very rapidly, too. Snelgrave's (1734) Introduction to his report on his second visit to Whydah gives figures. Only 33 ships left England for the West Coast in 1712; by 1725 more than 200 were counted. D'Elbée and Barbot record the disappointment of the Dutch of Offra, long-settled favorites of the king of Ardra, when no slaves were available. Five Dutch ships had to return empty to El Mina, while still others were waiting there (D'Elbée, 1671[II]:406). This was the chief source of the trading losses of the chartered companies whose enormous overhead rendered ruinous gaping descrepancies of timing. The competing goods of "interlopers" were mostly not only better but also almost thirty per cent cheaper. They picked up the slaves wherever they found them and thus escaped the hazards of an economic process transacted by means of an unsuited political setting.

D'Elbée's account of the early Ardrasian slave trade, when the native administration still attempted to cope with the tasks devolving on the center in direct dealings with the French, shows how formidable were the bureaucratic obstacles. His report of the transactions—ceremonial and commercial—between king and slaver, combined with the contemporaneous details of Barbot's account, give a picture of how great a burden it was for the foreign skipper to have to attend personally at Great Ardra whenever an arrival of another ship compelled him to pay again his customs and go through the complete diplomatic etiquette of a reception at the royal palace (*ibid.*:403 ff.).

The "rate in trade" with regard to slaves, says Barbot,

is generally adjusted with the king, and none is permitted to buy or sell until that is proclaimed; whereby he reserves to himself the preference in all dealings, he for the most part having the greatest number of slaves which are sold at a set price, the women a fourth or fifth cheaper than the men . . . no European must go there to trade, without waiting on him before he presumes to buy or sell. (1732:326)

And concerning Ardra in particular:

As soon as a ship arrives there from *Europe,* the commander or super-cargo must wait on the governor of *Little Ardra,* to be conducted by him to the king, taking along with him the usual presents, which commonly consist in a parcel of about three or four pound weight of fine coral, six *Cyprus* cloths, three pieces of Morees, and one piece of damask, for the King.

Tis usual for Europeans to give the king the value of fifty slaves in goods for his permission to trade, and customs for each ship.

The *Europeans* being obliged to deliver at their own charge, at Great Ardra, all such goods of their cargo, as the king has pitched upon for himself out of their invoices, . . . we always adjust the price of *European* goods, of slaves, and of the blue stones, called *Agry,* . . . with the King of Ardra; which being agreed on that prince causes a public crier to proclaim it about the country, and to declare that every man may freely trade with the super-cargo of such a ship, who is to satisfy the crier for his labour. . . . And without such public notice from the king to his people, none of them would ever dare to dispose of any *Agry* [pearls], slaves or blue stones above mentioned. (*Ibid.:*349)

The governor or his officers accompany the factor about four miles from the shore, where they appoint a house for him to drive his trade in. The factor then "causes all his cargo to be brought ashore and carried to that village by porters; and then . . . he sends up by them to *Great Ardra* all the goods the king has pitched upon for himself" (*ibid.*:349).

This is a greatly abbreviated description of the successive stages of gift-giving to the various strata of the king's sur-roundings—members of the family, commercial bureaucracy, ranks in political administration—and quite apart from the elaborate arrangements for the carrying of samples and staples at the various stages of the disembarkation. This gives weight to D'Elbée's complaint that the ceremonial of top-level trading negotiations had to be repeated by the foreigners whenever another vessel of theirs anchored off the coast and disembarked any of its personnel.

The alternative was to decentralize the process and to leave more powers to the vassals, relying on the tributary people of Offra, Jaquin, Whydah, Great Popo, or Porto Novo to support the king's officers. We have seen above the uncertainties besetting the domestic and external conditions of these tributaries, yet the total movement of the slave trade was embedded in the medley of these semi-independent bodies.

Close investigation reveals that only a spontaneous adjustment of these political organisms allowed the trade to be carried on. The small, weak, yet nominally sovereign state of Tori is a case in point. Maps aver its existence. Barbot (1732:327 and 345–46) and Bosman (1814) give geographical details. Tori was situated between Whydah and Ardra (inveterate enemies ever since the Houeda had their political capital at Savi), only nine miles from the sea and accessible to ships by river, but no farther away from Great Ardra, the political capital of Ardra. Indeed, an element of neutrality was present in many factual situations of the coastal area. Dual control was a frequent device. One and the same area, for example, was attributed by the European traders to Ardra and to Whydah (Barbot, 1732:327). In still other regions two commanding officers, acting jointly, were appointed by the contending parties; at still other times the commander was appointed by the two countries together; maps representing bush land employed the device of marking caravan access to Assem, next to Great Ardra, with the help of areas circumscribed by dotted lines, thus indicating swathes through the bush, a sort of shadow sovereignty, open to caravans over Ardrasian territory (cf. maps in Dalzel, 1793). Such improvised limitations of territorial exclusiveness may be regarded as approximations to the eventual solution, the port of trade.

The root difficulty of the inland states was, of course, locational. The center of administration lay, on the average, two days' distance from the coast. A further obstacle lay in the reluctance to permit travel by day to the stranger through a militarily threatened countryside; hence the inability of the inland empire effectively to extend its sovereignty to the coast.

The cumulative cost factors of delay and distance made patent the commercial inadequacies of the Ardrasian regime of the slave trade. There were the direct financial burdens to the slaver of the customs and tolls. Together with a multitude of conventional gifts these amounted one way or another to seventy-five or even eighty-five slaves—a value term—for each trading ship, whereas at Whydah they did not exceed thirty-two or thirty-five slaves "which is great odds in favor of the English and French factors residing there," Barbot remarks (1732:350). Even adding for Whydah another twelve slaves for transportation and similar costs, we arrive at less than fifty slaves compared with around eighty for Ardra, quite apart from an even greater disparity in the time lag of loadings.

The situation was thrown into relief by D'Amon's proposals of 1698 concerning a three-point treaty to be concluded between France and Ardra. Its second and third points referred to a monopoly of the slave trade to be accorded to France, Ardra moreover committing itself not to permit its citizens to make purchases from any country other than France. Ardra accepted both. But point one required a commitment of the king to transfer his seat to the neighborhood of the coast. This demand was not acceptable. The inland kingdom of Ardra refused to change its status into that of a maritime country. It can be stated with confidence that the rationale of the institution of the port of trade that was soon to be established in Whydah was neatly implied in the Sieur D'Amon's point No. 1: "Move to the coast!" (1935:83).

ON THE SLAVE COAST

When and how did Whydah replace Ardra as the slave port of West Africa? Ardra, an African inland state of archaic empire structure, had attempted vainly to run satisfactorily a novel kind of complex, large-scale world commerce. The sociologist might say with assurance that the situation imperatively called for an appropriate organ and that comprehensive change was inevitable. It falls, as ever, to the historian to show how the "inevitable" actually happened. The change required a state which was no longer of the inland type and which would speedily develop an impartial commercial bureaucracy. The social stratification which had to be improvised almost over-

night was conditioned on the possession of exceptional resources of natural wealth.

The argument of this book relies on the Gap of Benin for at
least a partial explanation of the shape of historic Dahomey
and stresses the climatic factor in that exotic geographical
accident. Nevertheless, we shall not be trapped into any crude
ecological determinism in regard to history. No more will be
assumed here than that the forms of human settlement, and
hence of state structure, do not remain unaffected by basic
ecology. Some economic effects of the meteorological conditions
adduced in Chapter Two will be our concern here.

Our seventeenth-century authors were enraptured by the
landscape that unfolded in Whydah. And the twentieth-
century scholars unanimously refer the exceptionally high level
of its statecraft and bureaucracy to the "garden of Whydah."
The Gold Coast—where gold was found or at least traded
widely—ended west of the Volta or just short of it at Lay. The
Slave Coast that followed eastward was an ambiguous term, as
Barbot had noted. In the stock exchange slang "Gynney-
Bynney" meant the Guinea Coast to Benin (Davies, 1957:39),
though, as Barbot (1732) said, even before reaching Benin it
loses its name. Actually, slaves were to be had right east of the
Volta, i.e., anywhere Ardra's coastal tributaries managed to
divert some of the slaves from the Ardrasian inland sources of
caravan trade. Whydah, with its lovely vista of parks and
pastures close to the beaches, dominated the picture. Actually,
right up to the western borders of Whydah, a good fifty miles
east of the Volta, the Slave Coast was as barren as most of the
Gold Coast, if not more so. Indeed, the Great Popos lagoons
were in evil repute as the homes of starvation. And again, east
of Whydah, the fateful humidity of the equatorial forest re-
asserted itself even before Lagos was reached. The coastal
regime created by the Gap of Benin comprised then no more
than the hinterland of *Whydah and Porto Novo, the only two
ordered and organized states situated on the coast between the
Volta and Benin.*

The territorially limited economic miracle, of which Whydah

was the center, was simply the result of a decrease of precipitation. A dry-hot local trade wind caused the annual rainfall, far from rising to an equatorial height, to drop to the level of the Northern Sudan. Cereals were at home again, millet thrived, and even maize flourished. Whydah was a large-scale exporter of food capable, in effect, of putting the militarily unbreakable Great Popos on a strangling leash of dependence for food. This abundance of crops caused an outburst of population growth as soon as orderly state building set in with the beginnings of the Ardrasian slave trade.

Two distinct groups of facts mark the two steps of causation: first, the ecological fact, a climatic advantage over the neighboring areas allowing for a local surplus of food; second, an external fact, the slave rush, necessitated a stratified bureaucracy and institutionalized the surplus. In brief, the Gap of Benin acted in two ways: as a lightning conductor for the movement of the slave masses induced by the far-distant tensions in the West Indian plantations and as the ecologic wellspring of a nutritional surplus which permitted an appropriate institution—the port of trade—to catalyze that supply into an essential factor of international commerce. Thus was the slave rush eventually formed into an event of overwhelming power that wrenched Dahomey from the traditional moorings of an African inland state and tossed it to exceptional heights of achievement.

Whydah's history was not only a contrast to that of Ardra *but also a continuation of it on the institutional level.* If an administrative method and a policy of neutrality were essentials of the port of trade, both were to some degree anticipated in Ardra. In a suborganized manner either principle *in nuce* was present there. Administration was operational in the setting of prices and in the manner of payment in kind, securing together a range of profit essential to the total process. As to neutrality, essential to international trading sites, we witnessed how in Ardra, entities which by their very nature were partisan, such as territorial states, produced devices of neutrality, such as joint controls or dual sovereignty. The transition of gold trade to slave trade was accompanied by an incipient change from a politically loosely knit trade area, as in Ardra, to a highly organized port of trade.

The rise of the Houeda tribe from obscurity had been slow (Dunglas, 1957:126 ff.). An offshoot of the South Nigerian peoples, the Houeda appear to have originated around the region of Lagos from whence they moved westward. Their longest sojourn was on Lake Hen (Atheme), abounding in fish, where a local Adja chief from the Tado branch may have attained kingship over them. Eventually they were driven from the lake and had to take to tillage, moving back nearer the coast. If we put kingship about 1520, this sums up their prehistory from the fourteenth century to 1671, when their king consented to Carolof's founding a village for the French West Indies Company. Carolof named it Pillau after his home in the Baltic lagoons of East Prussia.

By then the Houeda king had already taken a farsighted step, having separated from his political capital, Savi, in the north the village of Glegoy in the south near the sea as a prospective commercial center. The whole state territory was less than twenty miles across and showed no tendency to expand. It was still tributary to Ardra but making its influence felt, for instance, in Offra, a cotributary village.

J. B. DuCasse, the French empire builder coming from Benin and passing through Offra in 1688 found there in addition to a caboceer appointed by Ardra, another one put in by Whydah (the name that the village of Glegoy was to be given by the Europeans, after its Houeda inhabitants). DuCasse noted that Juda (the French spelling for Houeda) accounted for a very high annual number of slaves acquired by the English over the last two decades (1935).

D'Elbée's (1671) independent witness of twenty years earlier bears out some of these peculiar figures. In 1669, the king of Ardra undertook to provide, if needed, up to 6,000 slaves annually, an extremely high figure for that date. This may have been the occasion for the grand gesture with which

Louis XIV's admiral—his visit was memorable by his sovereign's gift of a golden carosse in which the king of Ardra rode into his capital—started that flood of slaves from the north from which, after the utter default of the French to supply the ships to fetch them, the English benefited, as DuCasse noted with surprise. The slaves Whydah sold to the English in Offra were the Ardrasian slaves destined for the French, notwithstanding that Whydah and Ardra were "inveterate enemies." And that perfectly timed condominium in Offra, also reported by DuCasse, may have been precisely the device by which Whydah made the grade, for our figures for Whydah subsequently move in that high range of slave exports indicated by DuCasse, though the purchases may relate to different national destinations and the ports handling the sales may have had varying puzzling arrangements between them. Our sources are discreet in those areas that might give away the rationale of those not infrequently paradoxical business moves to be met with in the slave trade.

The catastrophe of Ardra, scarcely fifty years after D'Elbée's auspicious visit, was only indirectly caused by any superior strength of Whydah, which at no time was a match for the manpower Ardra could mobilize. Through the tangle of personal rivalry and political intrigue that underlay the relationships of Ardra, Whydah, and Dahomey, in the long run it was the logic of economic efficiency that asserted itself. In spite of Ardra's preoccupation with the business rivalry of its everinsubordinate vassal, Whydah tended to ally with Ardra against the common enemy, Dahomey. Yet the military conquest of Ardra by Dahomey in 1724 was indirectly caused by the commercial efficiency of the port of trade of Whydah which, established some twenty years earlier, had eventually raised Whydah to the emporium of the slave trade both inside and outside Africa. The hard fact was that Dahomey had based its defense system on regular razzias that called for reliable supplies of arms, and thus Dahomey could not indefinitely leave the sources of its safety in the unreliable hands of Ardra, an archaic empire incapable of an effective administration within its own borders. Indeed, much before Dahomean might came down upon the Ardrasian empire to crush it, the pressures of a distant Western world began to focus on the weak spot of the new slave economy, which was Ardra. It was not the conservative powers of Portugal and Holland, who for centuries had been trading on the Guinea coast, but the late-comers, England and France, who precipitated Ardra's downfall in their eagerness to rationalize their West Indian plantations, which were growing into sources of enormous profit to the ruling classes of these two newest Western European powers. The new Whydah was, in effect, partly their creation.

Portugal had *de facto* monopolized the Guinea trade since the last quarter of the fifteenth century. The denominations of the cowrie currency, the names of the trade officials, the language of commerce were Portuguese, that *lingua franca* of a vast area. The emperor of Ardra had been educated in a convent on the Isle of Saint-Thome and his preference for the Most Catholic Monarch, the king of France, survived much awkward evidence of pedantry and red tape which hampered Colbert's efficiency drive. But all this antedated the slave rush. Even the local slave trade of the Portuguese, based on the Isle of Saint-Thome and Angola, was aimed at acquiring labor for Portuguese African sugar plantations and selling slaves to African inland traders on the Guinea Coast to transport their merchandise purchased on the coast from Portuguese hands. This built-in slave trade of the Portuguese in Angola was administered partly from Lisbon, partly through the local clergy and the monasteries. The African island plantations did not have at their disposal high-pressure governments such as those which directed the English and French chartered companies on behalf of West Indies plantations.

On the Guinea Coast the Dutch inherited the Portuguese trading system as well as the coastal forts which they had wrenched from them. The Portuguese knew no slave rush so keen on large numbers, quick delivery, and rapid return of their ships as did the later slavers. The trade of the slave rush was not any more Portuguese-Dutch in rhythm, but rather Franco-English. The decline of Ardra and the upsurge of Whydah take us into that more modern Franco-English period. Dunglas (1957) credits the small organized Slave Coast states of the eighteenth century with a greater consciousness of strength than either the interland countries of the Gold Coast or even Ardra had shown. Whydah and Porto Novo, he says, refused to concede monopolies of trade to any Western power, one of the reasons why the Portuguese and Dutch preferred the traditional methods of Benin, the Calabars, and Congo. Be this as it may, the crisis was sparked in Ardra by French action about 1669, and some thirty years later solutions in Whydah were brought to fruition by Franco-English military moves. This, then, was the actual manner in which the "historically inevitable" came about. The peripety which deserves a closer study was comprised in the years 1698–1704.

After many years of attempts to establish a viable relationship between France and Ardra, the Chevalier D'Amon made that formal proposal to the king, the first and foremost point of which he himself circumscribed as follows:

If the King wishes to see us established in his realm, it is required that the King permit us to settle on the coast, which would involve himself moving there together with the others of the capital, and that he make his residence there so as to attract trade, since otherwise the cost of transporting our merchandise to his present place of residence which is at a seven league's distance from the coast would involve us in ruinous expenses. (1935:83)

The king agreed to the granting of a comprehensive monopoly to the French on condition they undertook to ship at least 3,000 slaves annually while offering himself to deliver up to 6,000 slaves, should they wish, but the first and main condition concerning his changing of residence the king refused even to consider.

D'Amon's draft was dated 1698. In the early winter of 1701 D'Amon officially pressed the King of Whydah to set a firm price upon slaves: the king indicated that this would be seen to presently "when the French settlement was established" (*ibid.*: 106). The Wars of the Spanish Succession started and the powers that had settled around Glegoy (Whydah) found themselves in a state of war. Whydah, where the slave trade had flourished since the late 1680's, was now threatened by disruption. With the demise (probably in 1703) of the long-ruling monarch who was popular with the Europeans, the internal and external factors reacting against Ardrasian backwardness joined forces and brought about a veritable revolution. K. G. Davies, historian of the Royal African Company of England, records a distinct tendency on the part of the European slavers to congregate in Whydah after the turn of the century. By 1704 three great powers had forts and their main establishments there (1957:274). In the nature of things, international relations had affected the slave trade more than the gold trade. There was the award of the Spanish Asiento by Louis XIV to the French Guinea Company (September 14, 1701), which was to be administered by the farsighted DuCasse. Almost at once D'Amon pressured the king of Whydah, insisting on a stable price to be set on slaves.

Within the year the local garrisons of France and England took action on the issue of the domestic succession. Interventions of this kind, which the king of Whydah had practiced on the succession in the Great Popos, were this time made by the French and English jointly in Whydah. A few hundred European marines installed an enlightened ruler in the place of his less-appealing elder brother who seemed to suffer from xenophobia (1703). Not often do the natives' interests, as in this case, coincide with those of the foreign powers who happen to make use of their territory. But the national interests of Whydah strongly advised a disengagement of African affairs from the international conflicts which were impairing commerce. The quest for slaves, therefore, united the four powers in an effort to improve the services of their host, the king of Whydah, and to support him in his wish to keep foreign conflicts from his shores.

Two closely related steps must be dated with 1704—that of the Europeans' secret agreement to eliminate competition between them, and the proclamation of the new king, which declared the port and its environment "open" to all nations as well as a "neutral" in their wars. Davies quotes the English factor's confidential letters to his head office in London where tactful mention is made of the urgency of "entering into articles" with the French and the Dutch but never so much as hinting at their content (1957:274). In another context we will adduce our reasons to believe that a uniform markup on cost prices was at the core of the matter. An agreed handling of the "set rates" for slaves by the port of authority would help firmly to institute such "articles." D'Amon's demand for an established, unchanging slave price implied, of course, a "rate" that was uniform for all powers. But the "rate" also involved ways of payment, that is, a recognized standard. Actually it served as a basis for the fictitious unit of "ounce trade," that money of account of the slave trade.

By this time the separation of the political from the commercial capital—Savi from Whydah—was a fact. Phillips and Bosman still reflected a state of affairs where the king's palace of bamboo in Savi was the only center of business administration. The residence of the commanders of the foreign forts and their companies' warehouses together represented a closely knit agency of the port of trade. In Whydah, though a growing native town, the French, English, and Dutch forts were all in close proximity to each other while the native villages, each with their fetishes, were entirely separate from Savi. Whydah was still governed from Savi which also administered the countryside and whose officers proclaimed the food prices there. The French and the English attended to their arriving ships when these were signaled by cannon shots. The respective national flags were hoisted in response. The flagstaff was actually common to them. Such were things in time of peace. The king could count both on the powers arranging their affairs among themselves and on their support against Ardra, which after all controlled the supply of slaves, that *raison d'etre* of the whole substantial establishment at Whydah-Savi.

Colbert's *Compagnie de l'Inde de l'Ouest* (1664) was by now renamed *Compagnie de Guinée, chargé de l'Assiente* (1701). Commodore J. B. DuCasse had been present at the signing by Louis XIV of the Asiento treaty of that date. Among the new nobility attending the ceremony there was one Jean Doublet of Honfleur, the "Corsair of Dieppe," to whose role our story now turns. Only three years later, in September, 1704, we find him in Whydah, a man of astounding organizing ability. In that very year, according to Davies, the four slaving powers were moving their counters to Savi and with the king's permission starting to erect forts three miles from the beach. The young King Amar (or Amat), a great friend of the Europeans, had built for Doublet the fortress of Saint Louis de Glegoy.

In all probability the "articles" which the powers soon "entered" into committed them to a uniform practice of accountancy, i.e., how to set the "rates" at which their imported goods were to be priced in payment for native slaves. An agreement on a reasonable "markup" of, for instance, one hundred per cent on cost prices appears already to have been traditional in some parts of the Gold Coast. The proclamation of neutrality made by the king on September 6, 1704, might have made possible the swift price accord of the powers among themselves. Heavy fines against breaches of neutrality, coupled with the threat of immediate expulsion of offenders, irrespective of rank, offered further evidence of the revolutionary changes. Indeed, the break with Ardra might have made it advisable to provide for some expert trading personnel on which Whydah could, in future, rely for supplies. There is evidence that educated Islamic preachers, mullahs, professionals of the slave trade and traditionally trusted in Great Ardra, were solemnly invited to settle in Whydah. This literate and impressive type of international trader was to be an asset to the future port of trade. The date of this act of foresight was also 1704.

The next twenty-three years saw the organizational climax of Whydah's slave trade, the very success of which brought down upon it the conquest by the Fons of Abomey, the Dahomeans.

CHAPTER EIGHT

*S*avi: Sovereign Whydah and the Treaty

The tribal monarchy of the Houeda had made full use of the separation of "the political and commercial capitals," to use Édouard Dunglas' terms. The village of Savi was the political capital, the town of Whydah was the commercial capital of the kingdom, which was also called Whydah (Houeda).

The modest royal administration in Savi was carried on by a small staff of native dignitaries. Even the European diplomatic and military personnel was fitted in Savi into the compound of the royal residence. Normal status distinctions, largely hereditary, sufficed for the various functions involved in the household of a small state. This left room for the gradual development of a more elaborate establishment around the palace, which nevertheless remained in touch with both the native economy and the chartered slaving companies. Replace the native ruler seated in Savi by a Dahomean viceroy governing from commercial Whydah, and everything would have to be regrounded on new foundations.

The two capitals were an essential asset to the port of trade. Neither was more than a half-day's ride from the shore. The foreign fortifications in Whydah were grouped close together for mutual defense, providing for a safe communication between the beach, the native villages or "camps" attached to the various forts, and the military commanders' residences adjoining the royal residence in Savi.

Jean Doublet found the Houedan government of attractive simplicity. Six ministers, each with his personal job, were a model of bureaucracy on a homely scale. A gray she-ass carried one of the ministers—accompanied by his female musical retinue—to the food market, where he inspected the stalls and proclaimed the month's prices, announcing also the place of next month's market. This performed, the market turned into a picnic regaling the minister who sat down on the grass and fell to, also generously providing for the singers and dancers, leftovers being ignored for the benefit of the commonalty (Doublet, 1883:257–258; cf. also Bosman, 1814:487). Another minister checked on the currency: whether the cowries were accurately stringed and in full amount. If found short the string was confiscated by him (Labat, 1731[II]:163). In the markets lively bargaining on quality and measure was in order, provided there was neither rioting nor trickery.

The European commanders and factors in Savi formed a community regulating their own affairs under the supervision of the king, no one intervening between the monarch and the foreign dignitaries. As to naval affairs, a young native officer saw to shore and beach, port and harbor. The king's commercial aide acted as the head broker between native traders and European slavers. Dignitaries, officers, and the whole range of civil and military hierarchy were recruited from among Houedans. The king visited European friends alone and incognito in the evenings. The far from insignificant commercial wealth infused into a community of tillers of an exceptionally rich soil was absorbed by the community in an almost patriarchal manner. Bosman, the sophisticated Dutch governor of El Mina, repeatedly spent months in Whydah off duty, enjoying its people and atmosphere (1814:477). Indeed, our sources show the organic growth of Savi, how the village where the bamboo palace stood developed into the residence of the court of a small kingdom directing the slave trade into independent channels; how the Portuguese and Dutch traders drew closer to Savi; and how Savi was eventually transformed into the seat of the French company which took the lead in rationalizing the slave rush in a new kind of trading center.

Bosman, John Barbot, and Thomas Phillips had seen in Savi

a simple village undertaking governmental functions, yet only ten years later it was naturally fanning out into a diplomatic and administrative capital of an international port. This development had happened in the frame of a tribal kingdom, where popular custom and status provided the checks and controls that as a rule make bureaucratic hierarchy indispensable. Phillips described the pristine Savi, the king's village, thus: It contained about fifty "houses," the palace was the meanest he had ever seen, being of low mud walls, the roof thatched, the floor the bare ground, but near the king's palace on one side was "a town, consisting of about forty houses, walled round for the King's wives" (1746:232). According to contemporary sketches Phillips' "houses" were decent huts.

Commerce was initiated by the king in a conventional sequence. For the commander of the ship, the first day's official agenda was: what sorts of goods do we have and how many slaves do we seek to purchase? The second day's agenda was: at what price our goods and how much of each sort of good for a slave? The third day's was: presenting of samples of the goods and bargaining about their prices at considerable length. On the fourth day warehouses, kitchen, and lodgings were assigned to the Europeans. On the fifth day the customs were paid over to the king in goods at the agreed rate. Whereupon "the bell" was ordered to go about to give notice to all people to bring the slaves to the trunk to sell (*ibid.*:234). The bell was beat with a stick and gave a small dead sound. It was a hollow piece of iron in shape of a sugar loaf, with a cavity of the size to hold fifty pounds of cowrie. "Then the cappashiers each brought out his slaves according to his degree and quality, the greatest first" (*ibid.*:234). The captain of the "trunk"—the slaves' barracks—and the captain of the slaves were appointed by the king and together they were responsible for guarding them and having them transported to the shore. Each was paid the value of a slave for this service. Of the 1,300 slaves handled by them, not one was lost (*ibid.*:235). Only the Dutch had a presence in Savi with their three warehouses, seven chambers, and a garden. A stray Frenchman Bosman met found neither food nor shelter; indeed, he could not even manage to leave the country, since for several years no French ship had called.

Contrast this with Father J. B. Labat's (1731) map of Savi (end papers) which was based on the Chevalier des Marchais' sketch only twenty-five years later. The native village of Savi was now a mere background of a complex of palace buildings and warehouses, offices, gardens, and courts of the foreign factories, the heads of which had their commodious residences side by side with the palace. The picture shows French, English, Portuguese, and Dutch establishments. The French are served by a small daily market at their gate; there is also an open food market every fourth day with access for all; even a small hut is included for the comfort of female snakes who happened to be in parturition, with an armed guard in attendance.

A well-kept road linked the twin capitals, Savi and Whydah. Such were the amenities of the political capital and its courtly hospitality. Accordingly, there was a move on foot toward free trade and the institutionalizing of peaceful commerce. By 1704, however, three of the four powers which had forts in Whydah found themselves at war with the fourth, France. The seizure of enemy ships on the high seas was considered civilized practice; no merchant ship that left port was safe, its cargo being a lawful prize for the stronger craft, whether man-of-war or merchant man.

For Whydah this might have spelled the end of the slave trade. In this situation, King Amar summoned the commanders, as well as the chief factors of the powers, to meet him in the Hall of Audience of the palace. The king would not hear of their differences and insisted that trade should be free, not alone on land but also in the road stead and, indeed, even in the territorial waters (*à la vue de la rade*). Those who wished to trade should observe a complete neutrality and should engage their respective outfitters (*armateurs*) to accept responsibility, jointly and severally.

The opponents of France had reckoned on squeezing the

French out of business and rejected the king's propositions. He gave them one hour to make up their minds or else they would have to leave port forever, possibly forfeiting their goods. He conceded that the treaty should be valid only for a two years' term, after which it would need to be reconfirmed. The king solemnly declared that he would uphold the strict neutrality of the port of trade, taking his oath by the Great Serpent. (This deity was utterly foreign to Dahomey and native to Whydah.) In case of wrongful seizure, the head of the aggressor nation was made to pay damages in the amount of eight male slaves per foot length of the keel of the ship of the wronged party, the damage to be assessed in the presence of experts briefed by the king. The treaty bore the signature of Amar, King of Juda (Houeda), as well as that of Jean Doublet (the Corsair of Honfleur), and of the Chevalier des Marchais. It was given at Xavier (Savi) on the sixth day of September, 1704. The renewal of the treaty two years later bears the signature of a subsequent set of European trade dignitaries assembled in the audience hall of the bamboo palace.

Berbain (1942) makes no mention of the Treaty of 1704. Her reticence is in keeping with the dubious political status of the treaty, which obviously resulted from local French military moves. English historiography ignored it. The most recent French scholar to deal with the period—Édouard Dunglas (1957)—mentions our source patronizingly as "the good Père Labat." But he himself appears to have accepted the validity of Desmarchais' account reproduced in full by Père Labat (1731). In our own analysis of the rise of the port of trade of Whydah and the part played by the powers in settling the succession in and the neutral status of the new kingdom, we referred to the foreign intervention to which Savi owed its prosperity. However, the Annex to the Treaty of 1704 listing the price of a slave in the various trade goods (Labat, 1731 [II]:91–92) offers also, as we shall see in Chapter X, conclusive internal evidence of the authenticity of the treaty.

CHAPTER NINE

The Port of Trade Under Dahomey

The first century of Dahomean history was summed up by Frederick E. Forbes (1851), a visiting Quaker, as an almost continuous military struggle for survival. During that century, as we saw, momentous changes occurred in Whydah on the coast. The Houeda king in Savi was now independent of his former suzerain in Allada.

The port of trade organization established by the Houeda King Amar and a group of go-ahead European chartered companies in 1704 passed into the hands of the Fons of Dahomey, a people of fierce energy but lacking in all commercial experience. This amounted to the perpetuation of Whydah as an international port of trade under the aegis of an inland state.

Contrary to secular traditions of West African statecraft, as well as to the emphatic religious taboo of the sea, the Fons staked the existence of their state on the recently acquired maritime possessions.

The Alladoxonu had not underrated the magnitude of the venture. They were ready to uproot Houeda rule on the coast and to replace it by their own, while strictly avoiding any integration of this coastal lagoon area into their highly centralized state or any truck with the strange religious notions of its people. There was no room in the Dahomean pantheon for the despised snake worship of those ubiquitous fetish houses, nor any syncretistic tolerance of that great vermin alongside the heroic panther of Agassouvi ancestry. Moreover, no military strategy could be considered that ignored the taboo of the sea; even the employment of floats to cross rivers or lagoons was inadmissible. In the long run, no less radical solution to ensure physical safety and national morale was acceptable than the extermination of the bitterly hostile Houeda, their chiefs and leaders first, the remainder afterward, with their sale into slavery overseas as the only alternative. Events fitted this perspective. The destroyed royal residence of Savi was never restored; over and above the massacre of the Houeda in battle, 4,000 captives were put to death by the king in honor of the ancestral gods who had vouchsafed him victory; a few days later in the celebration of a feast another 400 Touffoes (of related stock) were sacrificed; the Houeda king, who had fled, was to be extradited by his own people to be put to death (Dunglas, 1957:155–57).

In addition to attempts to repopulate the country at large out of Fon stock, a wholesale resettlement of Whydah proper was undertaken. All this proves that with the conquest of the coast Agadja started out on a course of utmost daring, which was consistently followed up by his successors. It was the ruthless pacification of Whydah, eventually handing over the site itself to a European maritime power. Agadja took action. Bulfinch Lambe, the English factor at Jaquin, happened to be visiting on official mission in Allada when that city fell to the troops of Agadja, who took him to Abomey. After two years he was released with a gift of twenty pounds of pure gold and eighty slaves, having promised to return to Whydah with a group of English settlers (Snelgrave, 1734:66–68). Other English visitors were approached by the Alladoxonu rulers with a similar intent. Much later King Gelele sent a formal offer to the Colonial Office in London through Duncan, then English vice-consul general in Whydah. Duncan wrote the actual document, the king holding the tip of the pen. This happened more than a century after the seizure of Whydah, which the kings of Dahomey were neither willing to absorb into their realm nor endow with autonomy for fear of subversion and rebellion.

In the long run the cumulative military, demographic, administrative, and economic burden put a strain on Abomey. Military conquest alone of that tiny state of Whydah dragged on over another half century. Incursions of expatriate Houedas allied with Popos, terrible inroads of Oyo armies in support of coastal risings, insidious diversions started by various European forts whose artillery interventions resulted in bloody disaster for Dahomey turned Whydah into an open wound to the body politic. The improvising of the army of Amazons as a desperate tactical move during a military campaign and its maintenance on an admirable moral and physical level over more than a century are a measure of the energy that inspired the achievements. Only in 1772 was a lasting truce between Houedas, Popos, and Dahomeans arranged through the intermediary of the English governor, Abson.

The conquest of Whydah by Dahomey resulted in a twofold change. The Dahomeans disestablished the Houedan people as the bearers of a national state while perpetuating and developing under their own rule the port of trade organization initiated by that coastal people. Savi ceased to exist once Dahomey substituted its domination to the tribal entity of the Houedas. This involved a complete transformation of the government of that country, for, in terms of institutions, no less resulted from the replacement of the homegrown methods of a native society by administration at the hands of a foreign ruling stratum.

The occupation of Whydah and the running of its port of trade was a signal achievement of Dahomean statecraft, for the time-honored principle that coastal possessions are a peril to inland states had asserted itself emphatically. The occupation of Whydah was an act of military necessity; consequently, considerations of security governed the regime of the occupants in all regards. Any attempt to integrate the conquered province and its people into the tightly centralized administration of Dahomey might have disrupted that state. Also, the absorption of the Whydah religion into the tissue of religious beliefs and practices that sustained the social life of Dahomey on the popular level would have been fatal to the cultural unity of society. As administrative unification would have disrupted the state sphere, so any syncretistic unification of cultures would have struck at the foundations of the nonstate sphere of life with its religious roots. Security considerations in the widest sense, including the requirements of political and cultural unity, took precedence over commercial profitability.

For the future of the country was still far from secure. Even after a century of ceaseless wars aimed at broadening their base on the plateau of Abomey to the Oueme River in the east and the Couffo in the west, as well as to link up with the Fon of Savalou in the north, the situation of the Fon of Abomey still appeared precarious. Not only were they in a humiliating dependence from the cruel whim of the Oyo, great power of the northeast, but their contact with the recent European source of arms imports in the south had become uncertain, owing to the expansion of Ardra and the emancipation of Whydah from Ardra as a result of the permanent establishment of European forts on Whydensian soil.

It would be hazardous to guess whether the recurrent evacuations of the capital under the threat of overwhelming enemy forces also played a part in Dahomey's looking toward the coastal area for a safe retreat. There is evidence that at least once in the face of attacking Mahee forces the Dahomean army wavered between taking a stand and retreating to the Houeda territory. It eventually decided against the withdrawal for fear of being caught between two hostile fronts (Dunglas, 1957:161). In short, the pacification of Whydah could not be relied upon. The Houedas had permanent allies not only in the blood-relations settled beyond the Lake Atheme but also in the Popos who had not been subdued for good by any of their neighbors, as well as in the Europeans who never forgot the good old times of pre-Dahomean Whydah, with their intimate contacts with the sovereign in Savi, and above all the ample supply of slaves offered by the Ardrasian funnel and the easy dealings with the native caravans from the inland.

The metabolism of the new nation state, which based its defense on arms acquired through the instrumentality of annual slave raids, was under a grave demographic strain that time and again would issue in acute crises. Forbes's verbatim report of the post-campaign "self-criticism" held in the king's presence by Amazon and male army commanders shows the ominous implications of the institution of "annual slave raids" (1851[II]:86–104). The Amazon army, upholding its superlative level of soldierly qualities over the whole stretch of its existence, did not spare its own blood; nor did the king's generals spare their men's lives, their own heads being at stake unless they were victorious. In all directions and at all frontiers, surprise attacks were launched with the purpose of capturing those of active age and annihilating the old or disabled, a practice that spelled depopulation in the outlying acquired territories. Disaffection spread not only among the downtrodden and subjugated peoples, but equally in the ranks of the Dahomean soldiery, decimated in suicidal wars of revenge for aims often tactically unattainable. Members of the royal family, as well as unjustly degraded generals, occasionally deserted, accompanied by thousands of their best soldiers, thus swelling the ranks of an irreconcilable enemy. Yet the annual slave war was a national institution no king dared ignore, and, indeed, in the absence of any productive trade its discontinuation would have left the country without export goods for the purchasing of weapons and, therefore, defenseless in the face of embittered enemies who would not stop at selling his people wholesale into slavery overseas.

It was at this, the military and strategic point, that the country's inland status asserted itself incisively and made the conquest of Whydah a thorny problem. Inland status implied seclusion. It was a prime requirement under archaic conditions for military and strategic reasons. Both domestic and external policies hinged on physical apartness as a factor of safety. Except when favored by an impregnable geographical position, the core of a country was secured from hostile invasion mainly by distance, sometimes amplified by a zone of uninhabited territory or no-man's-land separating the habitants of otherwise contiguous states. If distance offered militarily some protection against aggression, it was chiefly because it made surprise attack difficult. Regular aggressive wars against neighbors, such as Dahomey appeared committed to, forced the country to a practice of surprise tactics with far-reaching effects on general policy. Wars were preceded by diplomatic campaigns intended to lull the victim into a false security; these were followed by the feint of the army leaving the capital in a misleading direction, eventually falling upon the enemy over secret byways revealed by treachery. The whole comprehensive maneuver involved long-term spying activities, often based on reports of blood-brothers in the guise of traders who had infiltrated the victim's area and kin group many months before.

The organizational frame of Dahomean Whydah was set by the office of the *Yavogan,* as the white man's viceroy and head of the civil administration. Later, in the nineteenth century, the chief representative of the Dahomean government in Whydah was the *Chacha,* an office that implied the absolute trust of the king. This post was vested by King Gezo (1818–58) in his white blood-brother, Francisco Felix de Souza, a man of exceptional qualities. His appointment appears to have removed from the *Yavogan*'s jurisdiction matters of foreign trade, concentrating them in the *Chacha*'s hands.

Effective control of foreign trade and the customs tariffs was secured by a set of regulations which enforced publicity of all actions relating to trade and created a network of automatic checks compelling a minute observance of the law. In broad outline, the bulk of business in the international port was unaffected by the change in sovereignty. Among these items were financial obligations of foreign traders for permission to trade in Dahomey, tolls and taxes due for exporting or importing slaves, and, finally, the prices of the slaves themselves. Instead of the king in Savi and his ministers as before, the *Yavogan* and the *Chacha* were now the final authorities, supported by a body of official traders, police, military personnel, and a host of porters, boat men, hammock men, and slaves of all sorts to do the rough work. As routine business, there was the general order of landing, the first meeting at the captain's tree, the sheltering of goods in tents on the beach, having them moved to a warehouse or a fort, the series of meetings with trade officials, the defraying of the customs to the king, and payment in goods at set prices for the usual services like watering, wooding, and so on.

Dahomey could not afford to take politicomilitary risks. Time and again officially provided services which introduced organs of supervision into all and every articulation of proceedings had to be used by the trader. There was no chance left here for uncontrolled contacts between individuals or groups not lawfully connected.

The strict separation of trade from war, of the military from the commercial personnel, was a further obstacle to politically unwelcome contacts. By such means all forms of contraband were prevented, particularly the smuggling of war materials; on the other hand, weapons could be channeled to friendly destinations. Also it facilitated the differential handling of imports of foreign companies, if so intended, as well as of native allies or dependent peoples. Similarly, the export of staples of various provenience could be given preference and monetary advantages secured to recipients. This would also make possible the creating of syndicates of exporters selected according to rank or status. Frequently the big men were allowed to sell their slaves at the favored "king's price."

Measures of stabilizing Dahomey's cowrie currency in terms of foreign exchange would also gain greatly in effectiveness through the complete control of external payments. The appropriation of gold by the royal treasury, for instance, could be effected with ease once the manner of foreign payments was dependent on the Dahomean authorities. The stable gold value of cowries may have been mainly owing to the existence of the port of trade and its strict methods of the controlling of the movements of goods. Admittedly, however, this would discourage native, non-Dahomean traders from frequenting a port, where the handling of all business tended to be to the detriment of outsiders.

The historian should now be prepared to draw the balance sheet of Dahomey's conquest of Whydah. Her monarchs were wary of being trapped into an integration of their conquest into the empire proper and preferred a remote control of the port, which was to remain insulated from the core of the country. There were, on the one hand, the slaves bartered for arms and the security this implied; on the other, the grave losses of female and male soldiers. The actual number of slaves exported from Whydah did not reach the level of pre-Dahomean times. Then the inland slave markets fed by many local wars served as a reservoir from which the caravans of the north and east filed toward the points of organized demand, while the surviving crop of captives from the annual war of one single state was now the only source of supply, and that supply was diminished by a heavy toll of the victims of sacrifices and a further reduction for the plantations of the king and the big landowners. DuCasse's estimate of 14,000 to 15,000 slaves annually bought by the English in Whydah in the years preceding 1687 may have been slightly exaggerated (1935:14); another 5,000 to 6,000 would surely have to be added for the Dutch and others, though much fewer for the Portuguese and French. Still, at the height of the slave rush an annual 20,000 slaves had been almost certainly exported from the Whydah area. It is very doubtful that the Dahomean period ever reached that level, since the transit caravans from the north and east, from the Mahee and the Yoruba, must have almost entirely ceased across Dahomean territory.

The vital asset, however, the inflow of guns and powder (as well as their denial to hostile neighbors), was now continuous. If Bosman could, several decades earlier, speak with horror of the number of European firearms with which he and his colleagues of all nationalities were supplying the inland natives, we need not doubt that Dahomey's prime purpose was attained. In her struggle for military survival she probably held her own only by virtue of the ample influx of arms from the coast.

Dahomey's long-run strategy was bearing fruit. The liberation of Dahomey from Oyo suzerainty was not due to Dahomey's own efforts. Still, she survived to see the day when external attacks from the north, first Nupe, then Fulbe, broke the power of Old Oyo in the first quarter of the nineteenth century. Dahomey's policies were vindicated.

CHAPTER TEN

Fictitious European Money in the Slave Trade

NATIVE AND EUROPEAN TRADING

From the first, trade between Europeans and Africans on the Guinea Coast developed in the framework of the immemorial trading procedures of the natives in the interior. It was not so much a case of mutual adjustment; of the two only the Europeans adjusted. The outcome was an uneven institutional development, very slow to begin with, but eventually leading up to an incisive monetary innovation.

Thorough reports on late seventeenth-century accountancy (Davies, 1957; Wyndham, 1935) convey the impression of a fateful vagueness in regard to profit and loss in the ventures of the Royal African Company. Its historian, K. G. Davies, admits the lag and proffers an anthropological explanation. "When one civilization trades with another," he writes, "their values eventually become roughly assimilated, but the process takes time, and it cannot be said to have been completed in Africa by the end of the seventeenth century" (1957:235). But while growth continued, the two trading systems remained apart. In the next fifty years the Guinea trade spread from Upper Guinea to Lower Guinea and thence to the Calabars; a miscellaneous bartering waxed into a substantial gold trade. If accountancy is the measure of advance in economic organization, progress was only very gradually made as trade was moving along geographical lines from west to east.

Davies' approach to the gap between West African and European trading ways ignores certain essential differences. These were institutional and organizational rather than valuational. Native trade was an import-directed activity of acquiring staples from a distance, bartered at the rate of 1:1. In emergencies simple variants of it occurred, such as 2:1 or 2½:1. European trade meant overseas exports of varied manufactures, oriented on monetary gain.

The native staples were standardized goods exchanged "in kind" against other staples, at traditional rates, by status traders whose income did not derive from the business in hand. The carrying, guarding, and negotiating was as a rule transacted by caravans voyaging over long distances. They traveled sometimes directly from one political unit to another, at times calling at semiannual fairs where they met with other traders.

If this is described as "administered" trade, its European counterpart should be designated as "market trading." In contrast to the former, it was bent on making a profit on prices, hence the need for a monetized accountancy to encompass a manifold of wares in a single currency, namely gold. A margin of sales over costs was imperative, since the trade could not be carried on at a loss even if the acquisition of gold or of slaves were declared its politically approved purpose.

To get at the heart of the difficulty, native trading had three strictly interlocking features which were unchangeable. First, its motive was the need for distant staples to be acquired for domestic ones. This was conceived as an act of barter of equivalents. Second, there was no intervention of money as a means of exchange. For even where moneys happened to be in local use, these would not have been necessarily current at both ends of the span. Finally, the rates at which the staples were exchanged were traditional and as a rule left no room for bargained prices. In the nature of things, these rates were determined by the same ecological, military, and transport factors which made for the trading of the staples in the first place.

The balance of adjustment had indeed to be borne by the European side. The absolute requirement of the Royal African Company's "market trading" with its inherent accountancy in gold could in no way be fitted into the native system of gainless barter at traditional rates. On the other hand, the Europeans could, and up to a point did, meet the native requirement of bartering "in kind" at a 1:1 rate (or a multiple of it) by a series of practical adjustments. How exactly this was done, and with what measure of success, constituted the history of the Guinea trade, including the era of the gold trade. Only the slave trade, reaching its height in the port of trade of Whydah, offered a solution to the European need for monetary accounting and a built-in profit margin.

A detailed chronology of the Guinea trade, as it proceeded along the coast, would show little or nothing in the way of progress in accountancy. There is no dearth of sources: Barbot's (1732) volumes, descriptive of quality and quantity of the wares that were traded from the northern limit of the Upper Guinea Coast to the southernmost tip of the Windward Coast, invited research into the records of the Royal African Company, since experts might confidently expect them to offer on the Gold Coast indications of adjustments in methods of pricing and cost accounting—but in vain. Many and varied standards of native trade were in use, sometimes even with locally changing rates, while European accountancy, to serve any purpose, would have had to reduce all items to one standard, namely gold. Yet, whether Senegambia or Gold Coast, Davies frankly admits that "the ledgers surviving from both regions give an incomplete and probably misleading picture of the profits and losses" (1957:238). Wyndham comments that the practical results obtained by the tentative adjustments of standards "were as diverse and perplexing as everything else connected with the African trade" (1935:70).

The "Bar Coast" is a case in point. The Africans' trade had produced here a method of rating and a corresponding accountancy of their own more advanced than in any other place. To quote Wyndham:

On the Windward Coast the "Iron Bar" was a measure of value to which all other goods were related, and the trade became known as "the bar trade." Thus when Moore was on the Gambia 1 lb of fringe, 2 lb of gunpowder, 1 oz of silver and a hundred gunflints were "bars." Each species of trading goods had a quantity in it which was a bar. The quantity, however, differed not only on various parts of the coast but even in adjoining places. (*Ibid.*:67)

No wonder that "bars" in native trade bore no relation whatever to European values even if the bar had "a static nominal value" of 5s., for the sale of goods to Europeans (*ibid.*:68). But the more systematic the valuation in bars was to the native, the more difficult it made European accountancy. The Royal African Company had to aim at a gold accountancy but was satisfied with using iron bars for a standard, which was not, however, uniformly related to gold in the various regions. European trade was, therefore, forced into the channels of a 1:1 exchange of staples "in kind." So long as bar trade was flourishing by rule of thumb, effective accountancy was out of the question.

Davies sums up poignantly the conditions in which the Guinea trade was carried on, saying that it was dominated by the natives' ways and needs. The main feature of European trade, as of Asian and later American trade, was a monetary profit-and-loss accountancy; yet in West Africa the Europeans had to relinquish this basic practice. All along and without exception they turned here to barter "in kind," native style, eschewing money use.

The *native* trade goods were gold, slaves, pepper, ivory, native cloths, and also hides, cattle, and millet. *European* trade goods were guns and powder, brandy, iron bars, occasionally coppers, Indian and European cloths, used sheets, hardware, ornaments by weight, and in course of time several hundred diverse items. The native trade goods served in different parts of the coast as standards. Of the European staples iron bars were the chief standard, as well as coppers in the Calabars; cloths ranked second. But European trade did not merely follow the pattern of native staple trading in general; over and above, whenever native and European standards had to be related, it was the native standard that was brought into play. In Senegal, for instance, the European goods were rated in hides, the slaves in bars of iron; but between these two standards, the European and the native, a rate existed of one bar of iron equal to eight hides, again the native good.

Also cowrie shells (*Cypraea moneta*) by weight or volume were European trade good, though serving also as a native standard on the Slave Coast. Cowrie by tale—one shell was worth one eighth of a farthing—as well as gold dust down to a speck, were used there as a means of exchange in the local food market. Gold was, of course, not a European but a native trade good, serving as a standard also in several regions apart from the Gold Coast.

Rating in iron bars, however, was not a privilege of the Europeans and scarcely contributed to the solution of their general problem of accountancy. Where the natives, as on the "Bar Coast," exceptionally employed iron bars as their only standard, they expressed the rates of all their staples in *bars* and those of most European staples as well. This may explain the fact, referred to by Davies, that only in the Windward trade could a profit-and-loss account in some cases be drawn up.

The exceptional case of the "Bar Coast" resulted from a vital feature of West African ecology. In contrast to prehistory in other continents, in most places in Africa bronze and iron came in together. This contributed to the eagerness with which European iron bars were in demand all along the Guinea Coast. Often these were also a standard in internal trading. Hence the list of traditional "bar" values with which the Windward Negroes confronted the English traders upon their arrival. The English again, mass exporters of "voyage iron," raised their coastal valuation of the iron bar so as to secure a profit where possible. As Davies says, "It must be explained that, though iron bars played an essential part in the trade of this region, the bar of account and the actual iron bar were not necessarily or always the same: (1957:238). In their "invoices" the Royal African Company valued iron bars at 4s.; with the natives in Gambia it had a nominal value of 5s.; in actual English trade "the value of the bar of account was generally 6s." (*ibid.*:238), while the iron bar cost only 4s. Wyndham (1935:48, n.1) even quotes a Parliamentary Committee for a proposal to reduce the normal value of the bar from 5s. to 3s.

Such an extreme "elasticity" of the shilling value of the iron standard might seem to have approximated an eventual common shilling reckoning of Africans and Europeans. But the advance which the modern student might see in such an approximation to a regional monetization was more apparent than real. It only proved how far the European standards still were from stability. Modern all-purpose money, which was to emerge a century later, was the outcome of market trading which was not yet even in a rudimentary form existent in the West African dawn of international trade. "The *bar* was not an effective medium of exchange as the term was understood in Europe," Wyndham says (*ibid.*:68). Even less were "shillings" more than a fictitious unit, not a means of exchange, though, like the natives' "static bar," they were serviceable as a local standard. The only exception, as we said, was for a time in the trade of the Windward Coast. "The practice was to allow to owners of hired ships a share in the Windward cargo," hence the accounts of the sale had to be cast up soon after the return to London. Between 1680 and 1687 "accounts have been preserved of ninety-five Windward cargoes, from which the profit of each voyage, clear of incidental charges, can be calculated" (Davies, 1957:239). The average profit was thirty-eight per cent. Unfortunately, there is no hint in what units profit and loss was accounted in the company's freight books (probably in £.s.d s).

The position in slave trading ventures was further vitiated by restrictions on the R.A.C.'s monopoly. It was valid only for the West Coast of Africa, invalid for the third leg of the voyage, from the West Indies back to England. But profits would be realized on that leg, which would bring to England the colonial produce for which the slaves had been auctioned in the West Indies. Also the planters paid off their debts to the Company only with a long delay; their payments "in kind," therefore, regularly missed the return trip of the boat that had made the two-leg trip.

Davies explicitly says that so far as the R.A.C. was concerned no profit-and-loss account of any single venture was on record. All the efforts of the R.A.C. at adjusting to African staple trade brought it no nearer a monetary accountancy in gold or an assured profit margin in its trading deals. It was a long haul from the initial settling of the physical measures of barter to European profit and loss accountancy.

"WEIGHT OF THE MEASURE"

The essential problem in any barter situation—how much of this for how much of that—was resolved step by step. The basic operational device was the establishment of the "weight of the measure." Agreement on the units on the one hand and the "fixing of the rates" on the other were the primary operations, since no trade could take place until both were agreed upon, and then no trade could take place *except at these rates*. No commercial significance attached to the establishment of the units of weight and of measure except that they offered the terms for the negotiation of the rates. In practice, as we shall see, units and rates were negotiated simultaneously.

Some passages from the account given by William Towrson, one of the first Englishmen to trade cloth for gold on the Guinea Coast (1555–56), illustrate how the units of weight and length and the rates between weights of gold and lengths of cloth were established in the early gold trade. At the opening of the first set of negotiations, it will be seen that the English offered a measure of two ells of cloth for a weight of two angels* of gold by sending both the English measure and weight ashore to the Negro "captaine." The latter sent back his own measure for cloth (somewhat larger) and his own weight for gold (a lesser weight) to show how he was prepared to trade. Thus two problems appear—to find identified units of the actual units of reckoning on the one hand, and a rate expressed in terms of these units on which barter was acceptable on the other. Trade carried on on these assumptions can be justly described as a 1:1 exchange. In the first turn

* An angel was one sixteenth of an ounce troy, or thirty grains.

. . . they sent a boate aboord of us, to shewe us that they had golde, and they shewed us a peece about halfe a crowne weight, and required to know our measure, and our weight, that they might shewe their Captaine thereof: and wee gave them a measure of two elles, and a weight of two Angels to shew unto him, which they tooke. . . . (Towrson, 1907:81)

In the second turn

they brought us a measure of two elles, one quarter and a halfe, and one Crusado-weight of gold, making us signes that so much they would give for the like measure, and lesse they would not have. (*Ibid.*: 81–82)

However, no agreement was reached at this place. At another place nearby the procedure began once more, the English offering the same rates. It is also indicated that a gift of two copper basins was included for the Negro captain at the opening of the negotiations. This "gift" belongs to etiquette, not to business.

When the Captaine was set, I sent him two elles of cloth, and two basons, and gave them unto him, and hee sent againe for a *weight of the same measure,* and I sent him a weight of two Angels, which he would not take. . . . (Italics mine. K.P.) (*Ibid.*:83)

The negotiations continued, now ignoring the gift,

. . . the Captaines had stooles brought them, and they sate downe, and sent a young man aboord of us, which brought a measure with him of an ell, and one fourth part, and one sixteenth part, and he would have that foure times for a weight of one Angell and twelve graines: I offered him two elles, as I had done before for two Angels weight, which he esteemed nothing, but still stucke at his foure measures aforesaid. . . . (*Ibid.*:84)

That is, the Negroes wished to receive, in effect, five and one-fourth ells of cloth for forty-two grains of gold, while the English offered two ells for sixty grains of gold.

The following day, after further negotiations, they agreed upon the measure and the weight, that is, the English ell and the Negro unit of weight of one angel and twelve grains.

. . . and when they sawe that the boates were ready to depart, they came unto them and gave them the weight of our Angell and twelve graines . . . and made signes that . . . they would take three elles. (*Ibid.*:85)

In short, gold by weight and cloth by length could be exchanged because an equivalence was established between a length of cloth (three ells) and a weight of gold (one angel and twelve grains), in this case using the unit of length of the seller of the cloth and the weight unit of the seller of gold.

Negotiated simultaneously were the units of weight and length on the one hand, and a rate between the units on the other, on a 1:1 basis. These were the fundamental operations through which the rest of the trade may be understood. The principle remained the same even if the rate involved a simple multiple of the 1:1 relationship. Cà da Mosto, sailing off the mouth of the Senegal, wrote in 1455:

In the regions of the dark-skinned Moors, they do not employ money. They do not know the use of it, and neither do the Negroes. Yet all the trade takes place by the exchange of one thing for another, often two for one. . . . (Cà da Mosto in De la Harpe, 1780)

More than three and one-half centuries after this puzzling statement was made, the English traveler Hugh Clapperton and his populous caravan found themselves in the Central Sudan short of subsistence in the vicinity of Bilma, north of Lake Tchad. The women of the region declared themselves unable to find a sufficiency of food and feed, but eventually undertook to offer what was required "at a 150 per cent profit." This passage of Clapperton's memoirs (1828) leads to the solution of Cà da Mosto's phrase of trading "two for one." The Bilma women stated the price as 2½:1 of the established rate or set equivalent. By 2:1 Cà da Mosto had meant double the traditional rate. In either case staples were operationally exchanged for staples but the rate at which the exchange took place was a simple multiple of the set equivalent. These two items of evidence, separated by a long stretch of time, turn out to contain, even though in a mystifying fashion, the underlying formula of staple trading: to the native mind the above was no else than a variant of trading at the set equivalent of 1:1.

SORTINGS

Trading staples 1:1 was the basis on which trade was carried on in Africa. From the first meeting of African and European traders on a tropical beach or on board a ship off an unknown coast, the elaborate procedure aims at this result, the mutual identifying of the units of weights and lengths that are customary with the other side. The result is a ceremonial commitment to the "weight of the measure." In trading cloth for gold this was the precondition of any agreement that could put the "rate of trade" beyond doubt. Without such a prime consensus on the language of trade the conversation could not start. And if the Guinea trade moving from North Guinea to the Gold Coast had ended there, nothing beyond the "weight of the measure" would have been needed to exchange most of the native goods for European ones. Even so, difficulties arose from two angles: partly from the growing variety of European export goods and even more so from the increasing number of slaves acquired on the Gold Coast. Indeed, the rush of the slave trade, which rose to a flood by the last quarter of the seventeenth century, created conditions for the European trader which could not be met without a development in the techniques of trading. And again the issue had to be resolved in the native style of trading, which was that of an exchange of staples 1:1.

Slaves were indivisible and of high relative value to the goods against which they were traded. Different European commodities in varying assortments had to be equated to a common standard before they could be rendered equivalent to a slave. From the native side warfare, clothing, ornaments, hardware, and an expanding range of needs demanded ever new European goods. Monetized accountancy called for a method of trading that transcended staple exchange so as to make room for profitability in the course of commercial dealings.

A new sort of staple was created which could be equaled with a slave in value and would permit the element of monetary accountancy to enter into the picture. This was the "sorting" of several staples which added up to the "rate of trade" of a slave. This term first may have made its appearance with the spread of the slave trade to the Calabars. The sorting was carefully selected to meet the needs and tastes of the slave-exporting "hands." The Africans' conservatism could not be ignored. A badly selected assortment was not made acceptable by reducing the price. Competition was directed solely toward the kind of staples offered and the quality of their make. While the king, apart from securing guns and powder, regarded the customs, tolls, and other monetary revenues to be derived from foreign trade as his concern, the population was keener on the quality and attractiveness of the goods than on any other feature of the bargain, including price. Nonetheless, the under-cutting of the R.A.C. by as much as twenty-five per cent to thirty per cent by the interlopers did not fail to gain favor with the natives. Slighter price reductions went, however, unheeded. Little room, therefore, was left to regular company traders for negotiating the rates.

Under these conditions no easy generalizations in regard to bargaining of the rates can stand. In the Calabars a local chief sometimes sold slaves that patently were bought by him in Central African slave marts up the river. He held out day after day for thirteen iron bars—instead of the customary twelve—and argued that inland price rises prevented him from yielding. The king of Dahomey, on the other hand, was notorious for his slave raids. His country produced no trade goods and had no other resources to acquire slaves but war. He was correspond-ingly readier to yield on the price of his slaves. Now, our sources insist on the king of Ardra, the king of Whydah (Barbot, 1732:326 and 349), and, in later Whydah, the *Yavogan,* the representative of the king of Dahomey, eventu-ally setting the "rates" of all imported trade goods. While hard bargaining on the part of the king is evidenced in regard to the goods "on which he picked," price was not the issue between king and skipper. Bosman (1814), who does not hesitate to reveal discords between the foreign traders and the king of Whydah, complains solely of the sovereign's inconsiderate preferences among the goods offered in pay for the slaves. Barbot (1732) denies any price competition of European traders among themselves and asserts that mode of payment

—what part cowrie, what part goods—was the sole matter of contention between the native and the foreigner.

It is certainly remarkable that over a period of much more than a century, under the rule of several kings and with a number of European countries involved, as well as hundreds of cargoes of slaves dispatched, in spite of grave incidents marring relations, difficulties are only rarely mentioned as arising on "rates of trade." Yet English and French sources alike stress the fact that the rates had to have the king's assent before trade could start with anyone but the king himself and his chief officers. Even for the earliest time, Doublet (1883) dwells on approved prices in local markets that are under the control of the king's officers. We do not doubt, of course, that slave prices were informally negotiated, that the private brokers could sell only at the set price, and that the European trade goods were sold in inland markets only at rates passed by the chief officers, by the Feoula in Ardra, the king himself in Whydah, or the local king in the Calabars. The answer is that prices in principle were unchangeable and the king merely took note, but did not negotiate. Gourg (1892) says they are unchangeable, except for iron bars and Indian silks. Change was mainly inhibited by the customary rule of the previous ship's rates being valid. Slave prices were a matter of high diplomacy in Dahomey and of lengthy negotiations in the Calabars, but on the rates at which the goods contained in the sortings were charged we have little information. We should assume that elaborate arrangements were made for the recording of the actual rates and particularly for the admittance of new goods into the sorting which usually caused a month's delay. The rest, it appears, was supposed to remain confidential, and we cannot be sure whether and to what extent the "rates" of the items in the sorting were in practice subject to bargaining.

Ancient laws were responsible for the categories by which human beings were valued. The Old Testament regulates the compensation which the temple can claim from adults redeeming their children or parents vowed to temple service (Leviticus, 27). Nachtigal (1887) found in Dar Fur (Eastern Sudan) roughly similar categories for a schedule of slave prices. Atkins gives a sorting for a woman slave at Sierra Leone in 1721.

		Gold Bars
1	Piece of Planes	10
7	77 lb. Kettles	26
3	Pieces of Chintz	12
1	Piece of Handkerchief Stuff	2
	The Price of a woman Slave	50

(1737:163)

Gold bars are described by Atkins as twisted pieces of gold wire, worth an ackey, or one sixteenth ounce of gold.

The items here listed as parts of the sorting formed an ideal, not a physical unit. The bill of lading listed the cargo irrespective of the manner in which the various goods were stacked in the hold for safety and the geographical sequence of the calls. On the other hand, the natives were familiar with the traditional goods and rates, many of the items being for sale at the storehouses of the companies. The companies took care to avoid competition by not offering the same goods, since they knew from experience that the supplies of gold and slaves were enough for all (Barbot, 1732:182).

The sorting was, as we said, primarily a device for maintaining in the slave trade the principle of trading 1:1 "in kind." Adjustments in applying that principle required practices as consistent as possible. Barbot (1732) tells us that the standard measure of a slave was "six spans from the ankle to the lobe of his ear." Isert says that

a young Negro must be four feet four inches in height [Rhineland measure] to be counted as an adult, and a Negress, four feet. . . . The amount by which they fall short of this measure is reckoned at 8 risdallers per inch. (1797:110–11)

A list of compensations was provided: ". . . for example, the absence of a tooth, 2 risdallers. If there are larger defects, such as the loss of an eye, a finger or other limbs, the deduction is much greater" (*ibid.*). If the slave was of substandard height or had a defect, the seller had to compensate the buyer. The sorting would remain intact. Its reduction would have left the choice of which items to remove and how to rearrange the sorting to the European trader. This would have constituted an infringement of the rationale of native trading "in kind," which implied the exchange of the sorting as a unit.

An operational device entered which again was strictly consistent with the principle of trading "in kind." James Barbot, Jr., in listing age groups and appraising them, starts with "the Black from fifteen to twenty-five years of age," i.e., the standard age. He continues:

from eight to fifteen and from twenty-five to thirty-five, *three pass for two:* Below eight and from thirty-five to Forty-five *two pass for one....* (1732)

The deficiency of being underage or overage is here operationally summed up and ironed out by a simple enumerational device.

The sorting was an ideal unit which relied on the good memory of the native and his skill in computing to keep up to the mark in a deal. This is perhaps where the famous damba bean came in as the saving device. Isert's (1797) inquisitive spirit and trained mind solved the riddle of the damba. *Abrus precatorius,* a widespread leguminous plant of Africa and Asia, has uniform and attractive beans, bright red with a black spot, hence also called "duck's eyes." The damba bean served as a unit of "medicinal weight," also for jewelry and precious metals. It was the popular gold weight of Dahomey. The large gold weight was the ounce troy of sixteen ackies or angels, these latter weighing twenty-four damba each. (In neighboring Ashanti a taku seed, equal to two damba, was in use.) Damba beans as such were worthless. Their mnemotechnical use for the native was as a counter in keeping track of the value of the trade goods owed to him for the gold he had sold to the European trader.

An ounce gold, equal to £4 (or 80s.), makes an ackie one sixteenth of £4, i.e., 5 shillings. On the Gold Coast, where the Europeans bought gold and paid in goods, a leather bag, containing the damba weight of the amount of the gold sold, represented the £.s.d. the Europeans still owed "in kind" to the native. In removing exactly the number of damba corresponding to the gold already paid off, the damba that still remained in the bag indicated the amount of trade goods owing to the native. Being familiar with the "rates" of the goods already paid to him, he would keep count of the goods coming to him from the trader. Incidentally, the absolutely stable cowrie-gold ratio enabled him to translate the damba with ease into cowrie amounts and £.s.d., as also into any silver currency such as Dutch guilders or Danish risdallers, kept stable by the Europeans at a gold rate.

If the sorting adhered to the native principle of 1:1 exchange "in kind," it also made room for the trader's commercial skill in introducing new products and offering the trade goods in the most profitable proportions. Though the amounts of the goods that were laid down as equivalent to an "ounce" were set out permanently, the selection of the goods that were cheapest at home was in the competency of the European trader.

The institutionalizing of a profit margin was still to be achieved.

ENGLISH "OUNCE TRADE" AND FRENCH "ONCE"

From the start the native monetary framework in which Europeans were compelled to trade hampered them in the monetization of their own business. Yet short of that, two essentials of Western foreign trade were lacking: an expanding variety of exports, the values of which can be added up, and a built-in margin of profit. K. G. Davies has shown how the absence of a reliable profit-and-loss accountancy undermined the capital structure of the Royal African Company and eventually forced it to relinquish the exporting of goods about 1712, long before the formal liquidation of the company in 1750.

Two questions sum up the issue in operational terms. First, already in the initial decade of the Company's trading no less than a hundred fifty (Bosman, 1814:376) kinds of European goods were traded in units of various dimensions—brandy and gunpowder by volume, iron bars and guns by the piece, cloths by length, and cowrie by tale, weight, and volume. How were the diverse goods to be "added up" prior to being exchanged for a few native staples? Second, how, in a trade carried on "in kind," were Europeans to avoid transactions leading to financial losses? More exactly, how was trading to be planned to secure a profit, and how was that profit to be realized?

A solution eventually was brought about by the introduction of the sortings together with a new unit of accountancy, the "ounce trade." And this happened without compelling the Africans to use European money, as nineteenth-century colonialism did compel them. Also, the adjustment was attained while operationally adhering to the accepted manner of native long-distance trading in West Africa.

The "ounce trade" can be traced back with the Europeans to a tentative monetization and the early attempts at protection against trading losses. Incipient monetization may be seen in the use the natives made of staples as standards, a practice adopted by the Royal African Company. The prominence of the iron bar in R.A.C. exports was, as we said, mainly prompted by the cultural bias of the natives for the use of iron. However, this submonetization was inadequate, because the valuation of iron bars in terms of gold was fluctuating, besides being different in the several regions of the coast. Into the Calabars "coppers," not iron bars, were introduced. James Barbot, Jr. gives us a list of copper bar equivalents in Old Calabar in 1699. These trade equivalents of the copper bar listed by him were not meant to add up to a unit of selected trade goods jointly offered for payment:

One Bar iron	4 Copper Bars
One bunch of beads	4
Five rangoes	4
One tankard	3
One bason No. 1	4
The other numbers less in proportion	
One yard of linen	1
Six knives	1
One brass bell, No. 1	3
The other numbers less in proportion	

(1732:465)

A rough marking-up of the iron bar acted as a commonsense precaution against loss. Captain Thomas Phillips bought them at 3/6 in London and sold them for gold at Bassam on the Gold Coast at 7/6.* This was an early one hundred per cent markup in the Gold Trade which was to be prophetic. It set the pace for the "average one hundred per cent" markup which was to lead to the introduction of a new monetary unit, the "ounce trade." The device of the "ounce trade" simply consisted in paying "in kind" for the gold ounces that the Europeans owed for slaves, but counting the goods in "ounces trade," i.e., with an average one hundred per cent markup. As this unit of accountancy gained acceptance by the native slave traders, the Europeans gained access both to variety in exports through monetization and to a built-in profit margin.

This history of the "ounce trade" was obscured by inadequate sources reflecting business data that, for understandable reasons, were largely withheld from the contemporary public. Parliamentary witnesses did not wish to appear as discounting the substantial profits accruing to the English economy from the slave trade, while maintaining that occasionally the slavers were made to pay excessive prices and were, of course, to be sympathized with to that extent.

Bosman left a hiatus in the printed text of his published correspondence, suppressing the figure of the actual prices of slaves and leaving a conspicuous dash instead. The history of

* "Each achy being about five shillings value . . . I took . . . for one iron bar 1½ achy (of gold)." (Phillips, 1746:214)

the "ounce trade" was not unaffected by such reticence. Parliamentary witnesses would offer elliptic information for reasons of tact, preferring to disappoint latter-day economic historians to causing, however unjustified, misapprehensions in the minds of contemporary black business partners. Nonetheless, ample evidence of the existence and justification of a change in the European traders' currency unit percolated.

For analytical purposes it might be useful to distinguish between three different terms referring to profits. First, the early practice of marking-up of staples *ex-ante* in order to secure a profit margin; second, varying levels of realized profits *ex-post;* finally, the emergence of a monetary unit, the "ounce trade" signaled by an "ounce" rated at 16,000 cowrie as distinct from the ounce gold which, before and after, was rated at 32,000 cowrie.

The inadequacy of our sources had long-term effects for historiography. Davies and Wyndham make no mention of the "ounce trade." Until recently it was ignored by historians of the slave trade, and even in the newest literature there is vagueness in discussing the issues involved. Newbury writes,

The price of slaves cannot be accurately determined, except in terms of the trade 'ounce'; and this unit of account, as on the Gold Coast, was made up of assorted European goods—cloths, cowries, beads, guns, powder, rum, tobacco and iron bars—valued locally in ounces, but varying greatly in their original purchase price.* (1961:22)

To begin with, the Parliamentary Committee of 1789 on the slave trade, inquiring into the mode of payment practiced in the West African trade, received unanimously the answer: "No payment, nothing but barter." Further questions confirmed the meaning of "barter" to be that payment was invariably in goods. Persons of authority, such as Dalzel, added that the payment amounted to only "about half" of the price of the slave. Another witness said: "A pound sterling would cost the European 10/–." Atkins, "a gentleman from Suffolk," who had

---

* Newbury's reference is clearly to the novel practice of payment in sortings. It does not even try to do justice to the distinction of ounce gold and "ounce trade," firmly established by Dalzel's and Isert's time.

joined the ship's complement as a surgeon, was more explicit. He wrote that in the slave trade at Cape Appollonia slaves were rated in "ounces" at four "ounces" each. "Allowing 100 per cent on Goods," he wrote, "they cost *at a medium* eight pounds sterling" (1737:74). That is, slaves rated at four "ounces" were paid for in goods costing only eight pounds sterling. While four ounces *gold* would amount to sixteen pounds sterling (at the rate of four to the ounce), four ounces *trade* (i.e., in goods) were equivalent to only eight pounds sterling. Put differently, the Europeans paid in goods marked up one hundred per cent the "ounces" which they owed. The "ounce" they paid was in fact what later authorities such as Dalzel called the "ounce *trade*" when its value was formally recognized at half the ounce gold, or £2.

It has been stressed by us that our one hundred per cent markup be understood as *an average*. The *ex-ante* markup varied for every good, and even for every transaction; yet the trader could hope to secure *ex-post* "at a medium" or "about" such a markup from its trade.

Admittedly, individual transactions or even whole cargoes might have yielded a much lower profit. Yet it would be preferable for the sake of clarity not to speak of different values of the ounce trade. The one hundred per cent markup was known at an early date and was noted by both Barbot and Bosman. Writing in 1680 of his purchases in the market, Barbot informs us that chickens cost "about sixpence a piece, if bought for goods, which is threepence prime cost" (1732:330; cf. also Bosman, 1814:503). In estimating the amount of customs fees paid at Whydah, Bosman remarked that the customs—which were paid in goods—"amount to about one hundred pounds in Guinea value, as the goods must yield there" (1814:489).

The "ounce trade," then, was a fictitious unit of account of a conventional value in the settling of European gold debts with the natives. Among themselves the Europeans called it "Guinea value" (Barbot) or, according to Wyndham, "coast money." The port of trade had signed a treaty with the slaver companies which recognized the payment for slaves in sortings by explicitly barring the king from insisting in payment in any *one* kind alone. Since cowrie possessed in Whydah the status of a trade good, this prohibition implicitly established the sorting as the sole mode of payment for the Europeans in the slave trade.

It is quite probable that the "articles" almost simultaneously "entered into" by the chartered companies' agents after 1704 in Whydah mutually committed them to the practice of an average *ex-ante* markup of one hundred per cent. Actually, for the *ex-post* markup the qualifying terms "at a medium" (Atkins), "almost" (Bosman), or "near" are never omitted in our sources. What we meet here is a transition from average markup to a new monetary unit. Dalzel's "Complete table of Dahoman moneys, numbers and weights, collected from the several authors" gives moneys as cowries by numbers and English coins by shillings and pence. There follows: "Four ackies = 16,000 cowries = 40s 0d." "J.F.," the editor of Dalzel's Table, remarks that there are two kinds of ounces: "the ounce *gold* worth four pounds sterling, and ounce *trade* of only half that value" (Dalzel, 1793:134). McLeod also gives its value as 40s (1820:90). Isert throughout follows the same practice (1797:112–13). As a witness before the Parliamentary Committee, Governor Dalzel was vague only on the price of a slave in Whydah, but consistently gave the prices in "ounce trade." He spoke of the "average slave" as costing five ounces (trade) = £10, while a "prime slave," when supply was low, was given by him as "little short of £30" (Parliamentary Papers, 1789:191).

The prices of trade goods, whether slaves or iron bars, were fluctuating, yet the cowrie rate of gold, as well as the gold value of the fictitious "ounce trade," was entirely stable.

When delving into the vicissitudes of the currency, we should not forget that the English Guinea trade never departed far from the institutional and operational traditions of the gold trade. Apart from a policy change on interlopers from 1698 to

1712—the ten per centers' arrangement—its whole history was comprised in the annals of the Royal African Company. Gold accountancy was not discarded in London, and with the English traders the "ounce" invariably meant an ounce gold, i.e., £4. The Mint in the Tower of London was the guardian of the validity of the standards of both gold dust and nuggets turned into bullion, with no more than a margin of one shilling either way. King and Court were subscribing shareholders in a venture which was expected to pay off in the regular business way, although, except in the early period, it did not. The Treasury could not be called upon to make up for losses, nor did it supply bounties per head of African slaves delivered in the West Indies. Shares in "Guinney & Binney" ventures were transacted freely; and in spite of some machinations and occasional corruption, the Guinea trade in its conservative ruts was placidly carried on, as disciplined by the inherent rigors of business life. Pilfering, bribery, and wastage of the employees' lives and morals never ceased to plague the Company. Yet for the economic historian the picture was unchanging; the English slave trade remained, on the whole, true to pattern.

French overseas trade and particularly the slave trade was organized by two groups, the courtly *compagnies* and the bourgeois *armateurs*. The undercapitalized *compagnie*, which provided sinecures for courtiers, usually lasted no more than a couple of years, only to be replaced by another ephemeral *compagnie* of a closely similar but not identical name which fared no better. The *compagnie* was responsible to the ministry for matters of naval and military concern: it was in charge of fortifications and warehouses on the Guinea Coast, employed the local personnel, checked claims for government bounties after African slaves landed in the French Antilles, and registered with the naval authorities the merchantmen, i.e., slavers, which required the permission of the authorities to leave port.

The *compagnies'* revenue was derived from a tax on the tonnage of every registered ship engaged in the Guinea trade. Their governors, managers, and other personnel had high salaries (cf. Davies, 1957:ch.i). Expenses conformed to the prestige requirements of persons representing the king of France. Of the officers on diplomatic mission during the century following upon DuCasse's tour of inspection (1682), we need only recall D'Elbée, D'Amon, Jean Doublet, Desmarchais, and in a minor capacity, the Père Labat and eventually the unfortunate Gouverneur Gourg to illustrate that they were representatives of the French government, not persons engaged in primarily private ventures.

As to the other group, very few wealthy firms of Nantes, the *armateurs*, equipped the privately owned craft which greatly outnumbered the *compagnie* ships. The bitter antagonism of bourgeois *armateurs* with their many shipowner-backers and courtly *compagnies* was a distinct contributory cause of the French Revolution, says Gaston-Martin (1931:433).

For institutional history, let us briefly return to the year 1704, the date when the efforts of the French resulted in the declaration of neutrality that established Whydah as an international open port. K. G. Davies uncovered the fact that in the next two years the English and French trading companies "entered into articles" (1957:274). In the English historians we find no hint of the dramatic events that were soon to take place in the bamboo palace of the king of Whydah at Savi, according to Desmarchais (Labat, 1731). The intent of the treaty of the sixth of September, 1704, which bore the signatures of the slave trade diplomats, may have corresponded to that of Davies' unspecified "articles." A few cardinal points may be assumed: that only payment "in kind" shall be practiced; that sortings, i.e., a manifold of trade goods in payment handled as a unit shall be continued, and that no payments for slaves shall be demanded to be made in one single good; that an average "markup" which was spread at the discretion of the parties over the different goods in the sortings shall be the recognized source of the Europeans' profits. However, the 1704 text mentioned outright only the point preferring sortings as payment, the others were merely implicit. Also, it should be assumed that the English made no secret of their reservations as to the validity of the treaty. But the French, who were treaty-minded, had the upper hand. The king of the new sovereign Whydah had been installed by them. The French "once" was a direct outcome. For its study we must fall back on the case of the French *compagnie* slaver *Dahomet,* almost seventy years later, whose ship's papers Simone Berbain has published for us.

The *"once"*—the French word—was the money of account of the French slave trade in Whydah, both for slaves and European goods, just as the "ounce trade" was for the English. But its operation, at least ostensibly, was not, as with the English, based on the gold ounce, equal to £4. Unlike £.s.d., the French *livre* was not based on gold and, therefore, the *livre* value of the ounce gold was not fixed.

The matter may be put as follows: the French, in buying slaves, paid in goods at native rates. Simone Berbain, the leading historian of the French slave trade in Whydah, noted that *"les transactions se règlent suivant une unité de compte fictive qui est l'once, divisée en 16 livres les noirs evaluant les marchandises de troc d'après un barême fixé"* (1942:68). The books of the French ship *Dahomet* (1772) reveal that equivalents to the *"once"* were used in the ship's day-to-day accounts regarding the purchase of slaves. The goods offered in trade conformed to a schedule of prices which never changed, so the French Governor Gourg stated (1892:769). However, he expected iron bars which depended on demand coral and silks which varied according to quality.

A typical entry in the *Dahomet's* papers for a woman slave rated at i *"onces"* runs as follows:

Person of seller and sorting	"Onces"
From Bouillon, 1 woman at 8 *"onces"*	
3 barrels of brandy	3
123 pound weight of cowries	3
[at 41 pounds to the *"once"*]	
2 pieces of handkerchief stuff	1
8 platilles	1
[a closely folded white cotton fabric]	_
	8

(Berbain, 1942:113)

The above sorting contains a remarkable specification in regard to cowrie. The item "123 pound weight of cowrie = 3 *onces*" conveys that 41 pound weight of cowrie equals 1 *"once,"* i.e., 16,000 cowrie. The specification, which is conventionally attached to cowrie, is expressed by weight, equating the value of the *"once"* with that of a physical amount of cowrie. The amount of 41 pound weight of cowrie is thus identified with the amount of 16,000 cowrie by tale, and consequently with the English "ounce trade."

Berbain, however, avoids any mention of the "ounce trade." Though its features are nowhere summarized in literature, its basic elements are, as we saw, documented by a number of factual items, such as the markup of iron bars; the equivalent of £4 for an ounce of gold; the cowrie value of an ounce gold at 32,000 and of an ounce trade at 16,000; or, in the simplest terms, that payment was made for slaves at halfprice, by paying "in kind" with goods marked up one hundred per cent.

Similarly to the English scholars, Berbain reveals limitations under which her research was carried out. As the title of her essay, *"Le Comptoir français de Juda (Ouidah) au XVIIIe siècle,"* says, its subject was the functioning of the Whydah office of the French slave trade. Its scope was deliberately restricted to the French slave trade as focused on Whydah. Not only the slave trade in the French Antilles was not to be treated, but neither was Whydensian slave trade other than French. The English establishment was, therefore, not considered, and the English "ounce trade" was ignored. This made the French monetary system the sole frame of reference for the treatment of the *"once,"* which logically resulted in always implying, yet never mentioning, the fundamental difference between the English and the French monetary systems.

The role of gold in the English currency system (£.s.d.) contrasted sharply with the independence of the French *livre* from gold, which was conceived of as being absolute. Yet in actual fact, that independence from gold, which left the *livre* a fluctuating currency, for local reasons *did not extend to Whydah and its French establishment*. Under conditions given by the slave rush, the French could not avoid, any more than could the English, trading by sortings with built-in profit margins. This again involved setting up a fictitious unit of account. The English, with their gold currency, anchored this fictitious unit in gold. Neither could the French in Whydah avoid doing so. Hence the paradox which confused Berbain's presentation. The French *"once,"* as money of account, was to maintain a stable cowrie value; that, by virtue of this fact, the stable gold value of cowrie would *indirectly link the "once" to gold* remained obsured.

Berbain also asserts that the value of cowrie was maintained only on the Slave Coast. This value was given as 16,000 cowrie or four cabess.* Indeed, it invariably occurs as *"once cowrie"* in the sortings recorded by the Captain of the *Dahomet*. By this fact the *livre* is also identified, namely as the sixteenth part of the *"once."* By inference the *"once"* equals the English "ounce trade" of likewise 16,000 cowrie. Briefly, the English "ounce trade" was worth half of the ounce gold and the French *"once"* was worth the same amount; yet this fact goes unmentioned in the definition of the *"once"* which is mentioned only as a fictitious unit, subdivided into sixteen *livres*. While the *livre tournois* was *not* on gold, Berbain's *livre* was indirectly bound to gold by way of the cowrie value of the *"once,"* of which it was one sixteenth. Hence no definite relation of these two variants of the *livre* was permissible, although the difference between them would have been fluctuating within a definite range, given by the actual rate of exchange between Paris and London.

Still another variant of the "ounce trade" which was closer to the English than to the French model was developed by the Dutch and the Danes. Its fictitious unit of the *"risdaller monnaie, or courant"* passed for half of the *"risdaller or."* These two were related as the "ounce trade" to the ounce gold.

The French *"once"* led in practice to a reduction of the number of items in a sorting to a very few trade goods,

* *"41 livres bouges ou 16,000 valent une once ou 4 cabèches."* (Berbain, 1942: 124)

reminiscent of Atkins' day. Berbain frankly states that for successful trading only three goods are required: cowrie, *platilles*, and brandy. The *Dahomet's* cargo consisted of up to ninety per cent of these. Isert's instances of sortings and cargoes point the other way: these include no less than a dozen trade goods. The number may seem irrelevant, yet it does lend support to the notion that port of trade, sorting, and "ounce trade" represented a triad in which the French *"once"* method of trading participated to a lesser degree. Indeed, it is doubtful that the feudal *compagnies* were eager to develop a greater variety of export lines to the extent that sortings in combination with the "ounce trade" permitted.

The unilateral introduction of a fictitious money of account, whether English, French, or other, was bound to cause serious disturbances in the economics of the slave trade. Analytically, the French *"once"* was merely a variant of the "ounce trade" with which it had much in common. The "ounce trade" itself was a derivation of that other innovation in the European trade on the Guinea Coast: the sorting. The sorting and the "ounce trade" formed an interlocking pattern that was destined to prevail right to the time of the intrusion of European currencies in Africa. On the face of it these European initiatives amounted to a one-sided revision of the rates of trade to the advantage of the Europeans. Out of the effects of the European initiatives two kinds of dislocations arose. Analytically distinct, the two strands of change were interacting.

Regarding prices and profits, the markup of European prices was definite. Before the slave rush, Thomas Phillips' iron bars, Atkins' reduction of slave prices from nominal pounds sterling to one half "in kind," and also Barbot's and Bosman's "Guinea value" and "coast money" (Wyndham, 1935:68) leave us in no doubt about the Europeans' business policy. Yet actual profits still fell far short of the one hundred per cent goal. The native seller of gold or of an occasional slave had not yet been faced with a complex assortment of goods but merely with a single import article.

With the slave rush, the changeover to sortings was rapid, and this, with the setting up of the port of trade, altered the very terms of barter. For unless rejected outright, sortings had to be accepted for payment as they stood. The average markup had consolidated into the "ounce trade" as a unit of payment. The discipline in commerce which emanated from the administration of the port of trade was a catalyzing element. That a slave, falling short in standard height or in limb or tooth, would leave the seller owing a deficiency payment was recognized in law, but not before the port of trade was administered by Dahomey would the merchant debtor be compelled, on the *Yavogan's* intervention, to indemnify the purchaser in cash, mostly cowrie (Berbain, 1942:72). The shelter offered by an open port amid international conflicts was sanctioned not only by the neutrality of the port authorities, but also by naval vessels.

The natives' first reaction to the "ounce trade" came in a spectacular raising of slave prices. Quoting K. G. Davies: "In the 'seventies and 'eighties the conventional price of an African slave was £3, this being the rate at which Petley Weybourne contracted to supply Negroes at Whydah in 1687." He adds in a footnote:

So far as I have been able to discover, all prices of slaves quoted represent the invoice value of the goods with which they were purchased. In most cases this invoice value was the same as the price which the company had paid in England, with no allowance made for cost of transport.

The text continues:

In 1963 the African Company's captains were instructed to buy what Gold Coast Negroes they could at up to £5 a head. After 1702, there were further increases, though possibly less marked at Whydah than elsewhere. Soon negroes at the Gold Coast were costing £10, £11 and £12 apiece, and in 1712 as much as £16 and £17 was being paid. Thus in the course of little more than twenty years the price of a slave had risen almost five-fold. (1957:237)

Institutionally, an intriguing fact remains. The natives still reckoned pounds sterling in ounces, and the "ounce trade" was used only by the Europeans. By 1791 the ship's papers of Captain John Johnston (1920) of the *Swallow* showed a slave price of thirteen ounces for average males, explicitly valued throughout in "ounces trade." However, there is nothing to show *any corresponding change in the natives' own money units*. We hold, therefore, that the natives' reaction has been primarily economic: an immediate rise of slave prices in the traditional ounce units. The increasing demand exerted by the French and the interlopers' competition has been hitherto offered as the sole—and inadequate—explanation of the sudden steep rise, without any reference to the "ounce trade." Unfortunately, the English witnesses of the 1789 hearings seemed not eager to clarify the price and currency turbulence in the slave trade, and merely reiterated that the terms of payment were very favorable to the purchaser. That exceptionally at least the English trader may have found himself induced to compensate the native seller for an excessive markup built into the "ounce trade" might account for Mr. Mathews' cryptic statement before the Parliamentary Committee: "We give them salt, some manufactures. £15 to £18 are paid over and above the invoice prices. . . ." (Parliamentary Papers, 1789). Thus far the transition is in terms of prices and profits. It seems a commonsense proposition that strains had to be met on either side with different expedients. Eventually, the Western adjustment, which broadened the avenues of growth and compensated the parties for the transitional losses suffered while withdrawing from untenable traditional positions, prevailed. Growth was many-faceted. The variety of European exports and of native cloths, the number and scope of inland caravans multiplied and so did the volume of coastal trade.

The institutional transition in the monetary field had three main stages. At the time of Petley Weybourne's stipulation of a £3 slave price, two standards, iron bars for European goods and cowrie for slaves, were current in Whydah. By 1704, the second stage, the king of Whydah had attained independence and foreign traders had to pay the "customs" to him. In the text of that year's "treaty," iron bars and cowrie were expressly replaced by the slave as the unit of value (Labat, 1731[II]:91–92). The pattern of the price list is familiar to us from countries practicing bartering of staples. The Laws of Eshnunna, dated earlier than Hammurabi's Code, had fixed equivalents in the manner practiced in our period on the "bar coast," namely, giving the amounts of the various staples that equaled one "bar" in value. In that Old Babylonian Law one unit of silver (the shekel) is offset against different quantities of grain, oil of different qualities, wool, and other staples in this same fashion. Since Whydah was to act as an international trade port for African slaves, the focusing on the slave as the unit of value appeared appropriate. However, very soon Dahomey took over and cowrie dominated. With this third stage, the pivotal point was reached. The stability of gold in terms of cowrie became the absolute requirement of Dahomey's overlordship. In the institutional field, study might, therefore, have to consider the pre-Dahomean period of Whydah, when iron bars for European goods and cowrie for slaves were the standard. On Dahomey's conquest of Whydah, cowrie became the standard for the value of the ounce gold. The economic upset was no more than the surface reaction to the far-reaching institutional changes represented by the emergence of the fictitious money units.

On a closer view we now confront the extraordinary fact that the gold price of cowrie had been maintained unchanged on the Slave Coast from the earliest pre-port of trade times over all the changes of monetary standards in Whydah, indeed, up to the French conquest of Dahomey. Bosman in the 1680's gave the value of 1,000 cowrie at 2s. 6d.; Barbot called the price of a chicken, which sold for 200 cowries, sixpence (Barbot, 1732:330). Both valuations lead to precisely 32,000 cowrie for one ounce gold. Dalzel's Table (1793:134 and n.; 135) fixed an ounce gold at four pounds sterling and an "ounce trade" at two pounds sterling, or 16,000 cowrie. The officer of the *Dahomet,* Crassous de Medeuil, as late as 1772 reckoned forty-one pound weight of cowrie repeatedly as equal with 16,000 cowrie, as being a French *"once"* or half an ounce gold (Berbain, 1942:101 ff.). In brief, the value of gold in terms of cowrie had formed part of the unchanging archaic monetary system of Dahomey.

PART IV

Conclusion

CHAPTER ELEVEN

Archaic Economic Institutions

SOCIETAL FUNCTIONS OF ARCHAIC MONEY

Our analysis deals with a West African instance of the manner in which the process of livelihood may be embedded in archaic economic institutions. Of the three exchange institutions, archaic variants of trade and markets have been already presented. Money, however, the stability of which was a singular attainment of the Dahomean economy, has scarcely been touched upon. What keeps the value of native money regionally stable and how are the equivalents maintained without any appropriate mechanism?

The answer, we suggest, is to be sought in the societal functions of money and their effects on the social structure. Take the variant of money here represented by the cowrie currency, and as a substitute for a market system look to the solidity of the structures that make up archaic society.

We shall call "archaic" such economic institutions as are absent in "primitive," kinship-organized society and emerge only in state societies, but fade again when money as a means of exchange becomes widespread. Economic institutions, then, that make their appearance in state societies fall roughly into two groups: those, such as the taking of interest, mortgage, or business partnership, which, once established, continue into modern times, and those others, such as voluntary work teams, the pawning of children, or the entailing of fruit trees, which eventually recede into insignificance or disappear. Only these latter, which are restricted to early state societies, deserve to be called specifically archaic economic institutions. They number several dozen, a few of which shall be listed. The antichretic pledge served a purpose akin to the taking of interest: the object given as a surety, whether land, cattle, or slave, was not only handed over to the creditor but the creditor was also entitled to use the object until the debtor had paid up. Sales were ensured even in the absence of markets: in parts of the Sudan sales were regularly held through brokers and even auctioneers were employed who often were also the brokers. For almost all staples equivalents were established in what we have called "staple finance," particularly in the operation of redistributing and household accountancy.

Exchange institutions such as trade, market, and money possessed their archaic variants. Notably this was the case in "administered" trade, involving the status trader or the port of trade; "isolated" markets with a compulsory money use; and last but not least archaic variants of money, of which the cowrie currency of Dahomey was an outstanding instance.

In general terms, money is a semantic system similar to speech, writing, or weights and measures. This holds good for all three money uses—i.e., for payment, as a standard, and as a means of exchange. Now, archaic money has the singular effect of solidifying the social structure. Institutions tend to be strengthened by the quantitative identification of obligations and rights resulting from the introduction of numerals. Sociological features to which institutions attach are mainly status and state building. Archaic economic institutions were, as a rule, mediated through their links to these two. Status is confirmed and the state is consolidated in the course of the development of such institutions, which, on the other hand, rely for support on interests benefiting groups and classes.

Specifically societal functions attach, therefore, to archaic economic institutions, apart from their strictly economic role. Ibn Batuta (1958) is to be credited with the discovery of the use of thin and thick copper wires as status money in the fourteenth-century Niger empires. Thin wires, in which wages were paid, bought only firewood and coarse millet, while the thick ones bought anything, not excluding elite goods. Limitations of consumption thus were set up for the poor, while the higher standard of life of the leisure classes was automatically safeguarded. Without unfairness one can here speak of "poor man's money" as an instrument of maintaining upper-class privileges. But status connotations of a deliberate welfare intent were also on record. In the sixteenth-century Near East, a "poor man's ell" existed in Basra, for the purchase of cheaper sorts of cloth. It was longer by a fifth than the regular ell with which the expensive cloths were bought.

The opposite bias prevailed in the "elite circulation" of Homeric Greece, in reciprocating gifts of treasure. In West Africa "elite circulation" was a principle of trade. Horses, ivory, skilled slaves, precious metals, jewelry, and treasure objects could be acquired only in exchange for items of this series of elite goods. In the ancient Near East status differentiations attaching to archaic moneys may serve as a key to some cuneiform economic riddles. According to the Code of Hammurabi, loans repaid in silver carried an interest of twenty per cent, while if the loan was repaid in barley, the rate was thirty-three and one-third per cent. Yet the mode of repayment was apparently left to the free choice of the debtor, which would certainly seem odd. If, however, as there is reason to assume, silver loans were accorded only to nobles, while the common man could expect only a barley loan, status would account for the apparent absurdity. It is evident that archaic money was in various ways connected with status, creating powerful invisible linkages in the social tissue.

COWRIE AND GOLD

Separate currencies operated in each of the three neighboring countries of Dahomey, Ashanti, and Whydah. In Dahomey units of cowrie shells were issued by the monarch; in Ashanti gold alone was current; in the port of trade of Whydah the English slavers developed the money unit of the "ounce trade" as a money of account, the French used the no less fictitious *"once,"* and the Dutch and Danish the *"risdaller monnaie."*

If the international gold standard of the nineteenth century rested on the pound sterling as the firmly established artificial money unit, on most of the Guinea Coast this function fell to

the Dahomean stringed cowrie. It was issued regularly in peace
and war, remaining stable both in terms of the domestic price
level and of foreign exchange between cowrie and gold.
However, the comparison of the roles of gold and cowrie must
not be strained. In the West gold served as a backing for bank
notes, and, through the foreign exchange rates, also as a
regulator of the mechanism of external trade. No such integrative tasks attached to the shells. Also, Dahomey possessed no
merchant fleet and carried on no active trade; and the shells,
which were its sole money, originated on distant coral reefs
from which traders could export them as ballast at a very slight
expense to themselves.

During the last three-quarters of a century, intensive research has been carried out on the uses of cowrie, both as an
ornament and as money. Conchology, geography, cultural
anthropology, archaeology, and economic history have contributed. J. W. Jackson (1915) has recorded the total range of the
prehistoric spread of cowrie. Only exceptionally were speci-
mens of the two money cowries found: others of the numerous
species of *Cypraeidae* were preferred by early man as more
ornamental or more stirring to the sexual imagination. Passing
from prehistory to early historical times, when iron, copper,
and the precious metals were used as money over wide areas,
cowrie appeared alongside the metals, but rarely, if ever, as the
sole currency. Historical cowries are only of the monetary
type, namely, *Cypraea moneta* and *Cypraea annulus*. The
heavier and larger *Cypraea annulus* with its bluish-grayish
shade and yellow-ringed body was usually mixed with the milk-
white, dainty *Cypraea moneta*. The place of origin of *annulus*
was the east coast of Africa opposite Zanzibar. This second-
rate cowrie reached Dahomey mainly by sea and had to
compete with the much handier and also neater *C. moneta*. In
any event, cowrie currencies nowhere show correspondence
with prehistoric finds in the same areas. Also, there is in
historical times, including antiquity, an absence of cowrie
money in the Near and Middle East in contrast to most of
West Africa and part of the Far East.

Currencies, with their institutional features, are a phenomenon far removed from the merely ornamental aspects of cowrie as a culture trait. This gives to the study of cowrie money that conceptual definiteness which lends fascination to economic history. A warning is in order against the ethnocentric bias that so easily takes hold of us on economic subjects that arise outside of our own Western culture. Over many centuries, silver and gold on the one hand, cowrie on the other, were in competition. Although in the Near East silver had been ahead of gold for at least two millennia, eventually modern man in his sophistication ranked gold as the winner. We will here disregard silver and restrict the comparison to gold and cowrie.

A rough balance between the native qualities of gold and cowrie that enhanced or reduced their respective suitability as units of currency may be appropriate. Among the indisputable advantages of shells over gold is their existence in recognizable units: gold has no units, being measured by weight, and at the time no acceptable units of gold weight existed. Another advantage of the shells is their minute unit value, which brings the vital item of primitive life, the mouthful of food, within popular reach, whereas gold with its elite connotation may be at a disadvantage, specks of gold dust in the Whydasian market notwithstanding. On the other hand, in its "industrial" use gold possessed an alternative employ of great economic importance, which derived from a highly elastic demand. The ornamental demand for cowrie is inelastic, and even within its limited range not of comparable economic significance to that of the "industrial" use of the previous metals. When it comes to the stability of a gold currency, the essential role of the industrial uses of gold are too well known to be stressed here. But to return to the virtues of cowrie, it cannot be counterfeited, whereas gold dust and gold bars are frequently adulterated by admixtures of brass dust, and gold coins are subject to clipping. Still another policy aspect recommends cowrie for its revealing of hoarded wealth through its bulk: the Spartans, aware of the fact that their leaders could not resist the lure of bribes, had to forbid the import of gold, favoring iron instead. King Gezo of Dahomey is quoted by Burton as saying that although there is gold in the neighboring Kong mountains, he preferred cowrie for two reasons—because it could not be counterfeited, and because no man can become secretly rich (1893[I]:117, n.3).

A physical quality of cowrie plays a part in its ambivalent fluidity. Cowrie shells can be poured, sacked, shoveled, hoarded in heaps, kept buried in the soil, chuted like gravel —they remain clean, dainty, stainless, polished, and milk-white. They are transportable in their tens of millions, which tends rather to impede the successful operation of a cowrie currency and, indeed, to cause already established cowrie currencies not infrequently to disappear again.

We are used to ranging cowrie with the other shells as a sample of primitive money in a supposed evolutionary perspective of the "origins and development of money." Historical research removes this evolutionary bias. Cowrie currencies emerged on the Middle and Upper reaches of the Niger at a time when metal currencies and, indeed, coined money were long established in the Mediterranean heartlands. This is the background against which the emergence of a new nonmetallic currency in Islamic West Africa should be viewed. It will then not be erroneously regarded as part of a general evolution of money, but rather as a feature in the spread both of centralized government and of food markets in the early Negro empires which left its imprint on the local history of money.

In the Dahomean area, gold dust and cowrie happened to be in close competition for the money role in food markets. The River Volta provided ample gold dust, and cowrie was available whether it had entered via the Guinea Coast in the south or the Niger region in the north. Gold also was found, as we know, in the mountains of north Dahomey. But gold dust could not be employed by males in the market, unless a fine balance (usually carried as in Ashanti by an attendant) was at hand. The Ashanti also used various nonstandardized, personal gold weights without common units. Whydah women were reputed to distinguish the qualities of gold dust and to be able to identify even a minute speck with their fingertips. However, this could scarcely compare with the discrete units of small change offered by the shells. In the food market cowrie won any time over gold. Moreover, it could be measured both by weight and by volume, not to mention count by tale. What proved in the long run cowrie's weakness, its extreme cheapness and volatility, was not fatal under archaic conditions. Cowrie easily held its own against European coins and succumbed eventually to the advantages of gold only under the conditions of international finance, for which it was utterly unsuited.

COWRIE FROM NORTH AND SOUTH

Well before Dahomey came into being, black and white met in West Africa on two fronts. The story of cowrie in Africa should then reveal some of the modalities of that meeting, first on the Middle Niger and, a century later, on the Guinea Coast. When, where, and how did cowrie shells penetrate West Africa? And by what agency was cowrie established as a currency system?

Dahomey was situated between the Guinea Coast and the vast Niger Bend. On the beaches of the Bight of Benin and on the Middle Niger, respectively, cowrie was infused by two different sets of traders—Berber Tuareg and later Arab on the one hand, Portuguese on the other. Their zonal fronts were, however, separated by more than a thousand miles, the distance between Timbuktu and Gogo, where the Venetians were dispatching the Maldive cowrie by Tuareg caravans, and the Portuguese in the south in Benin and Ardra, those outposts of Yoruba culture.

The earliest date by which cowrie can be presumed to have reached West Africa from the north is the departure of Marco Polo from Venice for his voyage to the Far East, about 1290. The surprise he expressed in a detailed account describing his meeting with cowrie money in southwestern China's province of Yünnan was not feigned. Our sources name Venice, Marco Polo's home and the domicile of the family business, as the agency that transmitted the cowries from the Persian Sea to the Niger, in order to purchase its gold with those exotic shells. This narrows the time range from 1290 to the spring of 1352, when Ibn Batuta found cowrie money in use at Gogo, on the Middle Niger, where the river sharply turned south. By all indications, in the empire of Mali cowrie was, alongside of gold bars and copper wire, by that time a regular currency, the gold rate of which Ibn Batuta unhesitatingly quoted by tale. He had been, like Marco Polo before him in Yünnan, much astonished at meeting with cowrie in the Far East, though unlike Polo he was thoroughly conversant with it and its use for money. He was struck to find that its value was as high as 1150 to a mitkhal, or gold ducat, which in the Maldives would fetch no less than 400,000 cowries, if not three times as much, which also happened, i.e., 1,200,000. The exchange rate in Gogo was mentioned by him with assurance. And Cà da Mosto, who had never seen cowrie in 1455 described *Cypraea moneta* correctly from hearsay and added specific information about their traject from the Persian Sea to Venice and from Venice by the desert route of the Western Sahara to the Niger.

The later date, when cowrie entered West Africa from the south, is almost as definite, though the medium of transportation by which this happened is much less certain. The Arab traders of the north represented the eleventh-century world movement of Islam (its seventh-century irruption had been quite brief and superficial). They were now keen to tap the sources of the gold that had been flowing since Roman times from the Upper Niger toward Carthage and Libya. Their cultural influence on the Upper and Middle Niger was paramount and cowrie, with which they were familiar from Arabia and India, was current in Mali, at least as far as Gogo in the east. The Arab trader was bred to the use of the mitkhal and its fractions, as well as gold and silver dinars and dirhems, and not limited like the "unbelievers" to damba beans and takus for their gold weights. When in the fifteenth and sixteenth centuries he was faced with the Europeans on the coast, his mullahs felt their equals in trade, if not their superiors.

Fifteenth-century Portuguese trade in Benin was a somewhat different proposition in the Arabs' eyes, who deemed it an intrusion into their inland territory. The Portuguese established themselves on the Gold Coast where they traded in the African staple, gold, for a limited number of European goods: cloths, guns and powder, used sheets, hardware such as basins and knives, but mostly iron bars and rings of copper. Neither caravan slaves nor cowrie yet entered into the picture. And with the opening of the sea route to India in 1497, Portuguese commerce changed direction. Based on the islands of Fernando Po and St. Thome, the Portuguese turned the Bight of Benin into a Portuguese lake. Their purchases from the natives were now intended for use in their local island sugar plantations and for coastal trading. This brings us back to the two regions where the Portuguese penetrated to some extent into cowrie-using areas: Benin and Ardra.

The insalubrious beaches from which Benin and Ardra themselves withdrew were not favored for settlement by the Portuguese either. They preferred the islands off the coast or inland fairs that lay about sixty or seventy miles from the sea. They induced the inland natives to trade the goods they had to offer, including slaves. But the superior civilization of Benin, heir to the religion, art, and statecraft of Ile-Ife, set narrow limits to Portuguese cultural expansion. Besides, the Arab traders from the far north would meet them there and bar further entry.

On Ardrasian matters, however, the Portuguese exerted a formative influence. The king himself had been brought up in a Christian monastery on St. Thome. A momentous feature of the cowrie currency resulted. The numerical denominations of that system, e.g., the designation of the smallest stringed unit of forty, the toque; the five toques of 200 shells, the galinha; the twenty galinhas of 4,000 shells, the cabess—all carry Portuguese designations. Important culture symbols such as the fetish have Portuguese names, as well as the administrative heads of any group or bearers of any port of importance, the *cabosseros*. It must be noted that the vernacular for the vari-

ous cowrie units was also current in Dahomey. Yet the Portuguese terms were employed over the entire area of stringed
cowrie money, including Dahomey itself.

Within a reasonably narrow span, sometime between the end
of the thirteenth and the middle of the fourteenth centuries,
cowrie then reached the Middle Niger; in the last quarter of
the fifteenth century the Portuguese may also have found it in
inland Benin. While on the Middle Niger it came undoubtedly
from the Mediterranean by way of the northern desert route,
its presence in Benin may have been due to seepage by Negro
or Arab traders from the Niger in the north. In any case, this
influx was later to be amply reinforced from overseas, rounding
the Cape. The trickle of cowrie shells from the east coast by
way of the valleys of the Congo may be ignored.

Our question regarding the origins of the cowrie currency in
Africa, consisting of loose shells at first, probably mixed
moneta and *annulus,* can now be partly answered. The when
and where of its arrival renders it a certainty that Dahomey
was *not* the originator of the cowrie currency system, although
it soon incorporated it and became its protagonist. Of this
crucial initial phase of a stringed cowrie currency in Dahomey
we know, however, next to nothing, except for the fact that
Whydah stringed its cowrie even before the Dahomean conquest. We have here in mind not the mere monetary use of
loose cowrie shells, but that organized system of cowrie as a
currency which, once it struck roots in Dahomey, became so
notable an instrument of its national existence and of the
regional economic organization over a wide area of the Guinea
Coast.

A recorded episode of economic history may be of relevance.
The Portuguese square cloth money stamped in Lisbon with
the royal arms of Portugal may have stimulated the monetary
imagination of the new inland rulers of the Guinea Coast.
Barbot's nephew, James Barbot, Jr., gave an intriguing on-the-
spot report of Angola, printed as a supplement to his uncle's
work about the Guinea Coast. Angola's secession from the
empire of the Congo gave the Capuchin monks the chance of

converting the natives and introducing an economic organization with domicile in Lisbon. A comprehensive taxation system
was based on the local administration which again was put in
the care of a privileged native stratum, the Sonassen. The
monetary systems of Angola were regionalized and were partly
made into a royal monopoly. The shells current as money, the
inferior simbos (*Olivetta nana*), were only partly of domestic
origin; others were imported from Brazil. Of the domestic
simbos, those of Loanda provenience were most valued for
their beautiful color. These favorite simbos were carried by
native servants in straw sacks, which held a load of sixty-four
pounds, to the Congo there to be exchanged for slaves and
square cloths of different sizes made of the bark of a native
tree. All things in Congo, James Barbot, Jr., wrote, are bought
with these shells, even gold, silver, and provisions, adding that
the use "of coin, either of gold or any other metal is suppressed
and forbid in all Congo, as it is in some other parts of Africa"
(James Barbot, Jr., 1732:518). The Portuguese government in
Lisbon, however, combined tax-farming with the monopoly of
the issuance of fiat money stamped in Lisbon and thence introduced into Angola at an excessive profit to the tax-farmer and
fiscal monopolist of this royal "mint."

The official value of the marked clouts (cloth money) was
four times the value of the unmarked ones, the double-marked
clouts being worth five to six times the unmarked clouts.
Except for fourth century B.C. and ninth century A.D. Chinese
experiments with paper money, no such ambitious schemes are
anywhere on record on an empire scale. The intellectual influence of the Portuguese on Dahomean state finance should then
not be underrated. The daring Guinean enterprise of regionally
stable moneys may have originated from previous Angolan
experiments. From the Niger empires of the north, greatly
antedating Dahomey, no hint of such a sophisticated currency
has reached us.

We must confess to ignorance of a more elementary kind,
namely how in the first place these shells came to be moved
physically in the mass from their homes along such vast

trajects. Traditionally, the migration of the cowrie was confidently traced by ethnographers to the Indian merchants' interest in monetary gain. But trade is no explanation, since it needs itself an explanation in terms of demand. Admittedly, the profit, in Ibn Batuta's terms, was in the possible range of 100,000 per cent. This, however, leaves untouched, the mainspring of the transaction, namely why specifically for currency purposes cowrie was so much in demand in Africa. Nor does it answer the question of whence the purchasing power was forthcoming, capable and willing to be spent on a large scale in such a manner.

The economist is indeed at a loss to account for the emergence in an early society of an effective demand of first magnitude for a means of currency as such. The notion that economic developments are mainly referable to what we have become used to calling "economic interests" is apt to be misleading. Rather, weighty events in the sphere of statebuilding and of economic organization may have accounted for the introduction of currency systems in West Africa. This may have been the source of the demand for money objects to be used as currency and consequently of the finance capable of supplying the purchasing power for their acquisition. The economic historian may have to seek an explanation in the rise of new empires, or even in the need for a popular currency which would speed the functioning of local food markets. Cowrie legend seems to point in this direction.

COWRIE LEGEND

Native legend on the coming to Dahomey of cowrie and of food markets connects the two events. Changeover from hunting to a settled life may have left natives without a place either in the kinship or the village organization. The distributing of food to the dislocated new subjects must have raised a problem for the Niger empires in the north, as it did later for the new bush and savannah kingdoms in the south. The latter may, up to a point, have followed the northern example.

One of the legends concerning Te Agbanli (1688–1729),

brother of Hwegbadja, the first king of Dahomey, tells of the circumstances of his settling in the Porto Novo area. One particular incident points to a close connection between money and markets. The narrator, recalling the time when there was no money, goes on to say that Te Agbanli "invented" a market:

> In those days there was no money. If you wanted to buy something, and you had salt and another man had corn, you gave him some salt and he gave you some corn. If you wanted fish and I had pepper, I would give you pepper and you would give me fish. In those days there was only exchange. No money. Each gave what he had to the other, and got from him what he needed.
>
> Now, as Te Agbanli was a stranger, he said to the people of Akono, "I see you have no market here. I want to invent a market for you."
>
> There was an Akono man there, who said, "Why should one give everything to a stranger? We gave him a place to live, and now he is asking for land for a market." (M. and F. Herskovits, 1958:364)

The unfortunate Akono man who raised these objections became the human sacrifice to consecrate the market.

At about the same time, Te Agbanli's brother Hwegbadja, the founder of the dynasty of the Alladoxonu kings of Dahomey, was engaged in a dramatic contest for power with Agwa-Gede, king of an autochthonous people, the Gedevi, on the southern reaches of the Abomey plateau. The two kings vied in the realm of magic and social innovations. Hwegbadja introduced a new code of laws, spinning and weaving of cotton cloth, burial of the dead in the earth rather than putting them inside trees, and payment in perpetuity by each succeeding monarch for the right to use the land for burials. "The people liked this very much. They said, 'all right. We like you. We will make you King for all time'" (*ibid.*:361). But though Hwegbadja won in the end, he lost out in the short run to Agwa-Gede. The latter king produced rain in a drought, "magic charm" locusts that ate the crops, a further charm to make the locust plague cease, produced the peanut from the earth and also cowrie money. The latter two events were intended as verification of his rightful status as king:

There was an herb called *tengbwe*. It sprang up at the moment. He [Aga-Gede] said again, "If the earth is truly my father's, then when I pull up this weed, a peanut will be pulled up with it." He pulled up the weed, and a peanut was there.

The people cried out. They put their hands over their mouths and acclaimed him.

He said again, "If the earth truly belongs to my father, if I pull up an herb, I shall see cowries." He did this, and there were cowries.

People now found food to eat, and no longer exchanged articles. They had money . . .

The people hurried to Agwa-Gede and declared, "You are our King. We have no other. . . ."

And so the people refused to recognize Hwegbadja, and it was only after the death of Agwa-Gede that Hwegbadja began to reign. (*Ibid.:* 366–67)

Cowrie money thus appears in the legend as an innovation of an autochthonous king. And the result—"people now found food to eat and no longer exchanged articles"—suggests a close connection in their minds between money and markets. Actually, as we know, Dahomean markets were food markets in which—a notable fact—cowrie payment was enforced.

The acting force that shaped and organized the economy was the state, in the person of the king. Food, money, and market are all statemade. The Hegelian-Marxian concept of a state as contrasted with the economic society (*Gürgerliche Gesellschaft*) of which it is only a function, is inapplicable to the early state. From Pharaonic Egypt and Babylon to the empires of the Niger, the state-building drive appears as a secular force within the sphere of economic organization. The factors that doubtless pressed toward statehood as such are a different matter. Together with the military factors, they belonged to the economic prehistory of the state. But once set on the course of state-building, the monarchy was engaged in the organizing of an army and its provisioning "in kind," the launching of a currency as an instrument of taxation, and the creating of markets and of small change for the distribution of the food. This again involved state-made "equivalents" which determined the rate at which staples could be substituted for one another in the payment of taxes and in rationing. These

performances of government concerning the economy are here
recalled from previous chapters to provide a more realistic
approach to the origins and functioning of the cowrie currency
which was strung by the king's wives in Dahomey for the provisioning of the conquered peoples in the local food markets.

COWRIE AND THE STATE

Primitive society knows not centrally issued shells for
money use; nor have these survived in societies where money is
common as a means of exchange. Indeed, Dahomean stringed
cowrie may strike us as an impressive archaic institution,
because the modern mind still grapples with some comparable
technicalities of monetary policy. While cowrie had vital welfare functions to perform, it was exceptionally hard to stabil-
ize. Grave obstacles had to be overcome in achieving stability
on a national and, indeed, an international scale.

Somewhat misleadingly, the dilemma might have claimed a
distant resemblance to modern welfare *versus* inflation alternatives. Owing to its infinitesimally small value, cowrie was over
centuries the money of the poor. Therefore, in India and later
(if to a lesser extent) in the Western Sudan, cowrie actually
served as an element of the welfare state, while its fluidity—
lack of viscosity—made the maintenance of a formal exchange
rate in terms of the precious metals as good as impossible.
Nonetheless, in Whydah and the whole of the Dahomean range
a perfect stability of cowrie in terms of gold was achieved
under the complex conditions of an international port fre-
quented by a number of trading countries practicing accountancy in gold or silver.

India's currency problems preceded those of West Africa.
The Moghul Empire visited by Ibn Batuta (1958) in the
second quarter of the fourteenth century displayed the utter
extremes of rich and poor but also what latter-day civilizations
would have described as an interest of rulers in the livelihood
of the masses. Ibn Batuta, having been appointed to a high
municipal post in Delhi, during a famine, had to shoulder the
maintenance of five hundred poor as a private person. In the

circumstances, cowrie formed in India a part of the Islamic-Hindu state's welfare economy. In Africa, under the Moorish administration on the Niger some four centuries later, conditions were not very different, except that—apart from Timbuktu where cowrie was still current—shells had been replaced by millet as the money of the poor. A reflex of the archaic popularity of the cowrie in the north might be seen in the Dahomean legend of the hunter's praise for the founding king who dispensed the threefold gift of peanuts, cowrie, and food market, all in one. Yet we have no knowledge whatever of the forces that moved the Fon dynasty of Dahomey to embrace cowrie money as a vehicle of empire building.

After Ibn Batuta had been in an important post for three years in Malan, the biggest of the Maldive Islands, he took his leave and was presented with a very large sum of cowrie by the king. He refused to accept the gift as useless to him in spite of the king's insistence that he could buy rice with it in Bengal, where he was going on his way to China. Batuta at first was inclined to agree, on condition that the king's officers accompany him and manage the deal. Eventually, he was given a sum in gold by the king. Other accounts also tell of cowrie as the money for which the poor could buy their daily rice, but which, even by the shipload, would not buy gold.

On the Malabar coast, which Ibn Batuta had also visited, gold and silver were the money of commerce, but in the inland towns of the subcontinent, cowrie was in use as the money of the poor. Cowrie was employed loose and was by no means subdivided into conventional denominations as in the Dahomean system. It is difficult to ascertain at what rate it exchanged against coined dirhems and if such exchanges existed at all, when and how the rate fluctuated. After all, even in the Maldives with its highly developed government that rate appears to have been extremely unstable, as Batuta recalled in relating his experiences in Gogo.

The contemporary West African empires began to import cowrie not later than the beginning of the fourteenth century.

It was a novelty on the Middle Niger and, although extremely cheap in India, by no means valueless in Gogo, where Batuta personally found it much appraised. Yet the Berber traders, who carried it one way on the long beat across the Western Sahara, insisted on payment in gold for carrying anything the other way. In the neighboring Central Sudan, cowrie was unknown, and during the famine the Moorish king distributed millet to the poor. Millet, besides being edible, bought everything in the market at a lower price than did any other currency. Like millet, cowrie money came to play a vital role in the welfare policies of the early state.

Technically, Dahomey's cowrie was definitely not primitive money. Paradoxically, it differed from the shell moneys of Oceania by being closer to the state of nature than the moneys of those "savage" peoples. The cowrie that was strung on threads was otherwise unworked and still in its natural condition as "harvested" on the coral reefs of the Maldives. The shells of the primitives were polished, cut, carved with skill and perseverance, often by strenuous communal labor. Hence the "scarcity" of their money. Its value derived both from that scarcity and from the emotional response to the human effort that went into its making (Malinowski, 1922). Cowrie, on the other hand, gained the status of a currency by virtue of state policy, which regulated its use and guarded against its proliferation by preventing shiploads from being freely imported. Neither in primitive society nor later under modern conditions (though for different reasons) was such a handling of cowrie possible. Bornu, in 1848, faced great difficulties in setting up a cowrie currency. Eventually, cowrie as a currency disappeared in Dahomey with the coming of the French administration, the introduction of metallic currencies, and the general use of money as a means of exchange.

In our terms, then, cowrie currency was emphatically an archaic economic institution. Its functioning deserves to be closely examined. The Dahomean rate of the seventeenth and eighteenth centuries was precisely 32,000 cowries for an ounce of gold (equal eight Arab mitkhals), while in the Sudanese region rates quoted by Heinrich Barth (1859), Oskar Lenz (1884), and Nachtigal (1887) in the middle nineteenth century fluctuated within 3,500 and 4,000 for a mitkhal (i.e., still very close to the standard). Nearer its origin, in the Indian Ocean, cowrie was almost without value, except by the shipload. Before the second half of the nineteenth century, the sheltering that was accorded by the great geographical distance from the place of origin operated against disastrous fluctuations of the rate.

All the more noteworthy were the lacunae in the geographical occurrence of cowrie in West Africa. Notwithstanding differences in other aspects of culture, many cultural traits, including many instances of primitive money, pervade an area and diffuse in all directions. But dispersion of archaic money in West Africa was quite different, and the distribution of its use was never general. In fact, cowrie-using areas and areas where it was not accepted for payment were as if their boundaries had been drawn by administrative authority. Admittedly, we are ignorant of the operational side of this "ecology of cowrie money," as one might call the phenomenon, which surprisingly comprised a rigid exchange rate between gold and cowrie often in fragmented but distinct areas. Hence the limited value of the attempts of mapping the areas of cowrie in West Africa in terms of a west-east boundary line dividing north and south: it was rarely found extensively employed in other than to some degree organized areas *and* along the trade routes. This again is explained by the nature of a caravan which possessed itself a traveling extraterritoriality as a semipolitical body, similar to the early state. For evidence of fragmentation: the city of Timbuktu, center of the gold trade, lying between the non-cowrie areas of the Sahara and the broad area of the northern Niger Bend, is known always to have been an enclave of cowrie money. Farther west, again, cowrie stopped short of the Atlantic Coast region. Nor did the area of its currency spread from the Niger toward the east into the Hausa states until much later. Binger, having passed through the cowrie belt of the southern part of the Niger Bend and the trade center of

Bonduku in the Upper Volta on the way to Ashanti, with the gold dust currency, made a note of the fact that the village of Aouabou was the last spot where cowrie still ran, the next village to the south refusing it (1892[II]:241).

Only under early state conditions, as in Dahomey, or in the caravans connecting state and state could the cowrie shell's excessive fluidity be neutralized. But outside the historical empires of Mali and Songhai, which antedated Dahomey, the vast areas of the valley and bend of the Niger had nowhere reached a level of statehood comparable to Dahomey. Hence the patchiness and the fluctuations, none of which existed in the realm of the cowrie currency of Dahomey, where it was an archaic economic institution. With the breakthrough of the world market, the fluidity of the shell got out of control again.

When these slick shells poured forth from the hold of ocean-going ships literally by tens of millions, cowrie had become a nightmare to the colonial administrator. After Bornu, in 1848, decided to introduce it, cowrie exports from Liverpool amounted in 1848 and 1849 to sixty and three hundred tons, respectively, i.e., together to 7,200 cwt; twenty years later, in 1868–70 its imports to Lagos amounted to no less than 172,000 cwt, equal, at the rate of about 380 cowries to the pound, to more than seven billion cowries over the three years.

In Uganda the British administration took action. In 1896, cowries were exchanged for about 200 for the rupee, but by 1901 the exchange rate rose to 800. After 31st March, 1901, cowries ceased to be acceptable in payment of taxes. At the same time the government placed an embargo on the import of cowries . . . having received information that large amounts were being imported from German East Africa. The Government's own stock was eventually burnt for lime. It was estimated that in 1902 after the destruction of the Government's stock there were still some three hundred million shells in circulation in Uganda. (H. P. Thomas and R. Scott, *Uganda*, 1935:231, q. Einzig, 1949:134)

In the French Sudan the French were fighting a losing battle against the maldistribution of the supply of cowries: "At Segou the French authorities accumulated at one time over twenty million cowries. . . . At Djenne (a distance of some hundred and fifty miles) . . . the Administrator . . . did not accumulate any" (Einzig, 1949:143). To relieve local shortage of cash in three villages, four million cowries had to be spent urgently in those communities by the French. Again, distribution was the issue" (*ibid.*).

By the end of the nineteenth century, cowrie had depreciated in Hausaland. C. H. Robinson's expedition had to sell a horse that fell ill and needed a few day's rest.

The trouble is, that we can not sell it, as its value in cowries would require fifteen extra porters to carry, to whom we should have to pay all the money they carried, and a great deal more besides. . . . (C. H. Robinson, *Hausaland*, 1896:46, q. Einzig, 1959:148)

The cowries had ceased to form part of an archaic economic institution without, however, becoming a commodity distributed by a market system that was not yet ready to take over. What, then, were the specific qualities of *archaic money* that produced societal effects which accounted for the near-perfect regional currency system of the eighteenth-century Guinea Coast?

STATUS AND STATE-BUILDING

Recent anthropological and historical studies have broadened our horizon in regard to primitive money. In the place of museum exhibits of exotic objects, attention is now directed to the institutions that invest the objects with the functions of money. Insight into the ranking of moneys on ethical grounds, as presented by Bohannan (1955;1959), brings to the fore the status-building function of money in primitive society. This aspect of primitive currencies gains in importance under the early state, along with their novel function of contributing to the creation of the state.

Archaic money was in effect closely linked with the evolving state structure. Alison Quiggin (1949) has shown how in primitive society the ceremonial presentation of staples by visiting tribes in the way of gift offerings to chiefs and kings endow the objects with *mana*. Utilitarian goods gain rank and dignity through their display as dues, tribute, or gifts of honor and their acceptance by the head of the community. Such impressive public dealings invest the goods with the prestige quality of money, the uses of which stand under manifold rules. She deems this to be one of the institutional sources of currencies, which, as we might add, introduce a quantitative connotation into rights and obligations, a condition that contributes decisively to the solidity of the social structure, thereby making it more resistant to the wear and tear of time and to the internal tensions that are inseparable from stratified state society.

A number of archaic transactions assumed the existence of statutory of customary equivalents, *as a moral safeguard against any, even though involuntary, profiteering.* The Jewish Mishnah showed a veritable obsession with the possibility of committing "usury," i.e., profiting through exchange. This again lent support to a legal casuistry in the Mishnah that distinguished pedantically between money and goods in all cases of sale-purchase, a procedure which would in principle exclude the purchase of money with money. Quiggin has empirically established her thesis that money is not, in primitive society, primarily a means of exchange. But neither was it in early state society, where it ranks among the building stones of the early state and its solid social structure.

Indeed, money as a means of exchange presupposes status-free money. Economic transactions such as sale purchase or renting-hiring are in traditional societies, as a rule, still accessory to status transactions, that is, goods follow the fate of persons. The appropriation by individuals, of land, cattle, and slaves is linked with changes of status, such as adoption or marriage. The transfer of use only instead of that of property is frequent, including even the mutual exchange of use, the property being retained by the families as in the *ditenutu* of the Nuzi of Babylonia. Also as a matter of status, land grants are linked to priestly, military, or trading posts. Thus, under archaic economic institutions, economic integration and status structure may be interdependent. The rights and obligations that flow from status may have integrative effects insofar as the privileges of some persons correspond to the negative status of others. Conversely, forms of economic integration may channel status effects, reinforcing them at the same time. This clearly holds good of redistribution, reciprocity, and household-ing in regard to their state-building and status links.

Exchange is no exception. Archaic variants of trade produce the status trader, whether the status is of kinship origin or by appointment. The port of trade is another such archaic institu-tion. Food markets that determined in large part the status of women are yet another. In such an institutional background, proceeding to archaic money, the cowrie currency of Dahomey moved into focus.

In the organizing of the economy, also, the early state be-longs to the archaic world of institutions. The economy of the state sphere and its administrative contacts with the state-free sphere shape the economic process as a whole. Again, when exchange forms of integration are present, the state plays a formative part. Equivalents in regard to rates of substitution and to the setting of prices, administrative ports of trade for imports and exports, compulsory money use in the local food markets are typical archaic economic institutions, which, at least peripherally, rely upon governmental functions. The peeling-off of economic transactions from the status transac-tions to which they originally adhered happens in the frame of statute law evolved in the state sphere. The dual focus of state and status thus shapes the development of archaic economic institutions, hence that close organization of society which is justly regarded as a source of archaic economic strength.

Bibliography

Atkins, John [R.N. Surgeon]
1737   *Voyage to Guinea, Brasil and West-Indies in His Majesty's
        Ships the Swallow and Weymouth.* Second Edition. London.
Baillaud, Émile
1902   *Sur les Routes du Soudan.* Toulouse.
Barbot, James Jr.
1732   in Appendix of John Barbot, *A Description of the Coasts of
        North and South Guinea, and of Ethiopia inferior, vulgarly
        Angola,* Vol. V. London: Churchill, Awnsham Comp.
Barbot, John
1732   *A Description of the Coasts of North and South Guinea, and
        of Ethiopia inferior, vulgarly Angola,* Vol. V. London: Church-
        ill, Awnsham Comp.
Barth, Heinrich
1857–58 *Reisen und Entdeckungen in Nord-und Central-Afrika in den
        jahren 1849 bis 1855.* Gotha: J. Perthes.
Barth, Heinrich
1859   *Travels and Discoveries in North and Central Africa.* New
        York: Harper and Brothers.
Basden, George T.
1921   *Among the Ibos of Nigeria.* London: Seeley Service.
Berbain, Simone
1942   *Le Comptoir Français de Juda (Ouidah) au XVIIIᵉ Siècle.*
        Memoires de l'IFAN, No. 3. Paris.
Binger, Captain Louis G.
1892   *Du Niger au Golfe du Guinée par le Pays de Kong et la Mossi.*
        Paris: Librarie Hachette et Cie.
Bohannan, Paul
1959   The Impact of Money on an African Subsistence Economy.
        American Journal of Economic History, Vol. 19, No. 4.
Bohannan, Paul
1955   Some Principles of Exchange and Investment Among the Tiv.
        American Anthropologist, Vol. 57, No. 1.

Bohannan, Paul
  1954   *Tiv Farm and Settlement*. London: Her Majesty's Stationery Office.

Bohannan, Laura and Paul
  1957   Tiv Markets. *Transactions of the New York Academy of Sciences*, New Series, Vol. 19, No. 7. Pp. 613–621.

Bosman, Willem
  1808–14 *A New and Accurate Description of the Coast of Guinea*. In John Pinkerton (ed.) *A General Collection of the Best and Most Interesting Voyages and Travels in All Parts of the World*, Vol. XVI. London.

Brunner, Otto
  1942   *Land und Herrschaft*. Brünn: R. M. Rohrer.

Bücher, Karl
  1913   *Die Entstehung der Volkswirtschaft*. Tübingen: Verlag der H. Laupp 'fchen Buchhandlung.

Burns, A. C.
  1929   *History of Nigeria*. London: G. Allen and Unwin Ltd.

Burton, Captain Sir Richard F.
  1863   *Abeokutia and the Camaroons Mountains*. London: Tinsley Brothers.

Burton, Capt. Sir Richard F.
  1893   *A Mission to Gelele, King of Dahome* (2 vols.), Memorial Edition. London.

Cà da Mosto
  1780   in De la Harpe, M. *Abrege de l'histoire generale des voyages*, Tome 2.

Clapperton, Hugh
  1829   *Journal of a Second Expedition into the Interior of Africa from the bight of Benin to Soccatoo*. Philadelphia: Carey, Lea and Carey.

Dalzel, Archibald
  1793   *History of Dahomey*. London: Author.

D'Amon
  1935   Relation du Chevalier D'Amon (1698). In *L'Establissment d'Issiny, 1687–1702*, Paul Roussier. Paris: Larose.

Davies, Kenneth Gordon
  1957   *The Royal African Company*. London, New York: Longmans, Green.

De la Harpe, M.
  1780   *Abrege de l'histoire generale des voyages* (Vol. 2, Ch. IV. Dahomey; and Vol. 3). Paris: Hôtel de Thou, Rue des Poitevins.

Bibliography 197

D'Elbée
1671   *Journal du Voyage du Sieur d'Elbée en 1669* par I. Clodoré. Paris.

Doublet, J.
1883   *Journal du Corsaire Jean Doublet de Hanfleur.* Paris.

Du Casse, J.
1935   Relation du Sieur Du Casse (1687–1688). In *L'Etablissement d'Issiny,* 1687–1702, Paul Roussier. Paris: Larose.

Duncan, John
1847   *Travels in Western Africa, in 1845 and 1846* (2 vols.). London: R. Bentley.

Dunglas, Édouard
1957–58   *Contribution a l'histoire du Moyen-Dahomey (Royaumes d'Abomey, du Kétou et de Ouidah).* 3 vols. Études dahoméennes, XIX–XXI. IFAN.

Einzig, Paul
1949   *Primitive Money in its Ethnological, Historical and Economical Aspects.* London: Eyre and Spottiswoode.

Foà, Édouard
1895   *Le Dahomey.* Paris: A. Hennuyer.

Forbes, Frederick E.
1851   *Dahomey and the Dahomans, Being the Journal of Two Missions to the King of Dahomey, and Residence at His Capital in 1849 and 1850.* London: Longmans, Brown, Green and Longmans.

Forde, C. Daryll
1960   The Cultural Map of West Africa: Successive Adaptations to Tropical Forests and Grasslands. In *Cultures and Societies of Africa,* Ottenberg, S. and P., editors. New York.

Gautier, Émile Felix
1935   *L'Afrique noire occidentale.* Paris: Librairie Larose.

Gourg, M.
1892   Ancien Mèmoire sur le Dahomey . . . (1791). In *Mémorial de l'Artillerie de la Marine,* 2ᵉ Série, Tome XX. Pp. 747–776.

Herskovits, Melville J. and Frances S.
1958   *Dahomean Narrative.* Evanston: Northwestern University Press.

Herskovits, Melville J.
1938   *Dahomey, an Ancient West African Kingdom* (2 vols.). New York: Augustin.

Ibn Batuta
1958   Travels, A. D. 1325–1354. Cambridge: Printed for the Hakluyt Society at the University Press.

Isert, Paul Erdmann
  1797   *Reize van Koppenhagen naar Guinea*. Amsterdam.
Jackson, J. W.
  1915–16 *The Use of Cowry-Shells for the Purposes of Currency, Amulets and Charms*. Manchester Memoirs, Vol. LX, No. 13.
Jobson, Richard
  1904   *The Golden Trade or a Discovery of the River Gambia and the Golden Trade of the Aethiopians (1620–21)*. Teignmouth, Devonshire: E. E. Speight and R. H. Walpole.
Johnson, Rev. S., S. J.
  1921   *The History of the Yorubas from the Earliest Time to the Beginning of the British Protectorate*. London: G. Routledge and Sons.
Johnston, Captain John
  1930   in *The Proceedings of the American Antiquarian Society*, N.S.
Johnston, Captain John
  1930   "The Journal of an African Slaver, 1789–1792," with an introductory note by George A. Plimpton. *Proceedings of the American Antiquarian Society*, N.S. vol. 39, pp. 379–465. Vol. 39. Pp. 376–465.
Labat, Père Jean-Baptiste
  1731   *Voyage du Chevalier des Marchais en Guinée*. Amsterdam: Aux dépens de la Compagnie.
Lambe, Bulfinch
  1744   Report, 27th November 1724. In *A New Voyage to Guinea*, W. Smith, editor.
Le Herissé, A.
  1911   *L'ancien Royaume du Dahomey. Moeurs, Religion, Histoire*. Paris.
Lenz, Oskar
  1884   *Timbuktu: Reise durch Marokko, die Sahara und den Sudan 1879/80*. Leipzig: F. A. Brockhaus.
Mage, Abdon Eugène
  1868   *Voyage dans le Soudan occidental (Sénégambie–Niger)*. Paris: L. Hachette et Cie.
Malinowski, Bronislaw
  1922   *Argonauts of the Western Pacific*. London: G. Routledge and Sons.
Martin, Gaston
  1948   *Histoire de l'esclavage dans les colonies françaises*. Paris: Presses universitaires de France.
Martin, Gaston
  1931   *Nantes au XVIIIᵉ Siecle, L'ère des négriers, (1714–1774)*. Paris: Félix Alcan.

McLeod, John
  1820   *A Voyage to Africa with Some Account of the Manners and Customs of the Dahoman People.* London: J. Murray.
Mercier, Paul
  1951   Les tâches de la sociologie. *Initiations Africaines.* IFAN.
Mercier, Paul
  1954a   *L'affaiblissement des processus d'intégration dans des sociétés en changement.* (Bulletin) de l'IFAN, Vol. 16.
  1954b   *Cartes Ethno-démographiques de l'ouest Africain.* Feuilles No. 5, IFAN.
Mercier, Paul
  1954c   The Fon of Dahomey. In *African Worlds,* D. Forde, editor. London: Oxford University Press.
Nachtigal, Gustav
  1879–89 *Saharâ und Sûdân.* Berlin: Weidmann.
Newbury, C. W.
  1961   *The Western Slave Coast and Its Rulers.* Oxford: Clarendon Press.
Parliamentary Papers
  1789   Minutes of the Evidence taken before a Committee of the House of Commons of the whole House to consider the circumstances of the Slave Trade.
Parliamentary Papers
  1790   Report of the Lords of the Committee of Council relating to the Slave Trade (Board of Trade) 1789. (Published 1790.)
Phillips, Thomas
  1746   *Journal of a Voyage to Africa and Barbadoes,* Vol. VI. London: Churchill, Awnsham Comp.
Polanyi, Karl
  1944   *The Great Transformation.* New York: Rinehart.
Polanyi, Karl
  1947   Our Obsolete Market Mentality. *Commentary,* Vol. 13, September. Pp. 109–17.
Polanyi, Karl
  1963   Ports of Trade in Early Societies. *The Journal of Economic History,* Vol. XXIII, No. 1, March.
Quiggin, Alison H.
  1949   *A Survey of Primitive Money.* London: Methuen.
Richard-Molard, Jacques
  1949   *Afrique occidentale française.* Paris: Berger-Levrault.
Robinson, Charles Henry
  1896   *Hausaland.* London: S. Low, Marston and Co.

Rodbertus, Karl
    1865   Zur Geschichte der römischen Tributsteuern. *Jarbücher für*
               Nationalökonomie und Statistik, IV.
Rostovtzeff, Michael
    1932   *Caravan Cities*. Oxford: Clarendon Press.
Roussier, Paul
    1935   *L'établissement d'Issiny, 1687–1702. Voyages de Ducasse,*
               Tibierges et d'Amon à la côte de Guinée (publiés pour la
               première fois et suivis de la relation du voyage au royaume
               d'Issiny du Père Godefroy Loyer). Paris: Larose.
Sik, Endre
    1961–63   *Histoire de L'Afrique Noire, Tome* I–II [Traduit par Frida
               Lederer]. Budapest: Akadémiai Kiadó.
Skertchly, J. A.
    1874   *Dahomey as it is: Being a Narrative of Eight Months' Resi-*
               dence in that Country. London: Chapman and Hall.
Smith, William
    1744   *A New Voyage to Guinea.* London.
Snelgrave, Capt. William
    1734   *A New Account of Some Parts of Guinea, and the Slave*
               Trade. London: J. J. and P. Knapton.
Thomas, Harold Bekan, and Robert Scott
    1935   *Uganda.* London: Oxford University Press.
Thurnwald, Richard
    1916   *The Bararo.* Memoirs, *American Anthropologist*, No. 4.
Towrson, William
    1907   The First Voyage of Master William Towrson, 1555. In
               R. Hakluyt, *The Principall Navigations of the English Nation.*
               London.
Wyndham, H. A.
    1935   *The Atlantic and Slavery.* London: Oxford University Press.

Index

Abomey: 5, 24, 26, 30, 35, 58, 95

Ackey (gold bar): 152

Administration: duality of, 53–54; government; 53–55; provincial, 55; role of women in, 56

Agadja, King: 24, 29, 132

Agriculture: organization of, 37–39; policy, 38–39

Allada: 10, 24, 131

Alladoxonu (dynasty): 14–16, 28, 131, 132, 185–86

Amazons: 8, 28, 30, 37, 52, 53, 55, 57, 133, 135

Ancestor worship: 54, 76–78

Angel (gold weight): 146

Angola: 19

Annual Customs: 33–36, 40, 51, 91

Archaic economic institutions: definition of, xxiii; Chapter 11, pp. 173–94

Ardra: 15, 19, 21, 24, 26, 27, 101, 105–06, 181; geography, 107; organizational difficulties of, 107–08; European intervention in, 108–09; Great Popo rebellion against, 111; commercial inadequacies of, 114

Armateurs: 160–61

Army: 36–37

Ashanti: 8, 10, 22, 28–29

Atkins, John: 152

Bar Coast: 142–43

Barbot, James, Jr.: 182–83

Barbot, John: 26, 92, 108, 112, 114, 142, 150–51, 168

Barth, Heinrich: 92, 190

Basden, George T.: 84

Benin: 5, 8, 10, 12, 19, 22, 121, 181

Berbain, Simone: 18, 93, 130, 162

"Best Friend": obligations of and to, 67–68

Binger, Capt. Louis G.: 84

Bohannan, Paul: 192

Bornu: 189, 191

Bosman, Willem: 26, 92, 102, 108, 109, 127, 150, 168

Burton, Sir Richard F.: 35, 40, 50, 83–84, 92, 93, 178–79

"Bush king": 57; economic functions of, 58

Cà da Mosto: 148, 180

Calabars: 19, 121, 150, 151

Castle trade: 102

Census: population, 41–43; as basis for tax assessment, 41–44; pigs, 43–44; cattle, 44; goats, 44; sheep, 44

Chacha (Minister of Foreign Trade): 136

Clapperton, Hugh: 148

Cloth money: 182–83

Colbert: 17, 124

Compagnies: 160–61

Compound: 10, 72–73; inheritance and succession in, 73–75; land rights in, 75

Copper bars: 155–56

Coto: 108–09

Cowrie currency: 93, 137–38, 173, 194; mythological origin of, 184–85; in India, 187–89

Cowries: 29, 40, 50, 83–84, 144, 164–65, 174; purchasing power of, 92–93; value of, 168; gold price of, 168–69; stability of, 176; history of, 176–77; advantages and disadvantages of, as money, 177–78; trade in, 179–80, 184–85; as welfare money, 187–89; geographical spread of money, 190–91; depreciation of, 192
Craft guilds. *See So.*
Credit: lack of, 85
Cult house: 78, 79
Currencies: multiple, 29
Currency: stability of, 92–93, 95

Dalzel, Archibald: 49, 159, 168
Damba beans (monetary weights): 153
D'Amon, Chevalier: 105, 115, 121, 122, 161
Davies, K. G.: 122, 140, 161, 166
Dega (Hunting chief): 45
D'Elbée, Sieur: 112, 118–19, 161
Descent groups: 71
Divination: 78
Diviners: 77
Dokpwe (Labor team): xxii, 60, 61, 62–63, 64
Doublet, Jean: 106, 124, 126, 151, 161
Duality (organizational): in government, 53–55; in army, 55; mythological basis of, 57
Dual numeration: 85–87
DuCasse, J. B.: 118, 122, 124, 160–61
Duncan, John: 92, 94–95, 132
Dunglas, Édouard: 12, 121, 130

"Elite circulation": 175
Equivalents: xvii, 49, 168, 186, 194; customary, 49; royal, 49; imported goods, 49; monetization of, 50; establishment of, 146–48

Fa. See Divination
Factors of production: xvi
Fon: 26, 125

Forbes, Frederick E.: 55, 92, 131
Forges: as shrines, 47
Free enterprise: xv
French Guinea Company: 122
French West Indies Company: 106

Gap of Benin: 3, 5, 17, 22, 28, 105; climate of, 6; geograpical influence of, 116–17
Gaston-Martin: 161
Gautier, Émile Felix: 10
Gbe (Mutual aid group): xxii, 62, 65–67
Gelele, King: 50, 63
Gezo, King: 26, 30
Ginger: 39
Gletanu (plantation): 38, 70, 88
Gold Coast: 11, 101, 102–05; European diplomatic relations with, 104–05
Goldsmiths: 90
Gold trade: 146–48, 159–60
Great Popo: 8, 27, 110–11, 116
Ground nuts: 40
Guinea trade: 18, 140

Hausa: 10
Hawkins, John: 19
Herskovits, Melville J.: 10, 34, 63, 71, 84, 85, 90
Hoes: forging of, 46–47
Honey: 39
Houeda: 131–32; 134
Household royal: 52, 53
Householding: xviii, 32, 70
Hunting: 45

Ibn Batuta: 174, 180, 184, 187, 188
Ile-Ife: 11, 12, 181; dynastic history of, 12–13
Iron bars: 144
Iron manufacture: 45–46
Ironworkers. *See* Smiths
Isert, Paul Erdmann: 153, 159, 165
Ivory Coast: 11, 104

Kana: 58
Kankie: 83, 85, 93
Katakle: 9

Ketu: 12
King's wives: 52
Kposi (Leopard wives): 54–55
Kumasi: 5

Labat, Pére: 129, 130, 161
Labor: xiv
Labor market: absence of, 62
Lambe, Bulfinch: 30, 132
Land: xiv; tenure, 70–71
Lenz, Oskar: 190
Little Popos: 108–09
Livre: 162
Louis XIV: 104, 124

Maize: 39
Mali: 10, 191
Manioc: 39
Market: system and mechanism of, xiii, xiv, xv, xvi, xxi, 32, 94; system, lack of, 81; "bush," 83–84; trade, 141
Marketplaces: xix
Markets: xiv, xx, xxi, 40; commodity, 32; consecration of, 40; cooked food, 81–83; effect on mobility, 82–83; set prices in, 83–84
Mawu-Lisa (Divine twins): 57
Merchant class: xiv
Mercier, Paul: 5–6, 10, 32
Millet: 39
Mishnah: 193
Monarchy: organization and functions of, 33
Money: definition of, xvi, 174–76; all purpose, 145; status, 174–75, 187–89; status building function of, 192–93, 194
———: fictitious, 140–69; effect of, on slave trade, 165–66

Nachtigal, Gustav: 92, 152, 190

Once: 162–63, 174; sample of, 162; compared with ounce trade, 162–63; cowrie value of, 163; *livre* value of, 163–64
Ounce: gold, 154; gold equivalent, 158

Ounce trade: 123, 154, 155, 156, 174; advantages to Europeans, 156–59; effect on slave prices, 166–67
Oyo: 3, 5, 11, 12, 22, 24, 27, 30, 59, 133; cavalry, 24

Palace: description of, 52–53
Palm oil: 39, 53, 88
Palm wine: 39
Passports: 47
Pawns (human): 68–69
Pepper: 39–40
Peto: 83, 85, 93
Phillips, Commander Thomas: 93
Pigs: 39
Planning, economic: 40–44
Plantations: 17, 18, 120; need for slaves, 18
Platilles: 165
Polo, Marco: 179–80
Popos: 133
Porters: 47–48
Porto Novo: 8, 10, 27
Port of trade: ix, xvii, xix, xxiii, 99, 174, 194; historical background of, 99–101; organization of, 28
Portugal: trading influence of, 120
Portuguese: influence on trade, 181–82
Pottery: 90
Price: xvii; mechanism, xxi; setting of, 87–88; changing of set prices, 90–91
Priesthood: 78–79
Profit: xv.
Pseudo-commodity: xiv
Public works: 51

Quiggin, Alison H.: 192, 193

"Rate of trade": 149, 151
Rates of exchange: xix
Reciprocity: xviii, xxiii, 32, 60–61, 62, 65
Redistribution: xviii, xxiii, 32
Religion: economic balance of, 79–80; consumption of revenue, 80; organization and function of, 81–83
Richard-Mollard, Jacques: 6

Risdaller monnaie (Dutch and Danish): 164, 174

Rostovtzeff, Michael: 100–01

Royal African Company: 18, 21, 27, 122, 140, 141, 142, 143, 145 146, 150, 154–55

Salt: 39; collection of, 45–46

Savi: 123, 128; separation from Whydah, 123; government of, 126–27; commercial ritual in, 128–29; foreign settlements in, 127–28, 129

Senegambia: 19, 20

Shrines: 78

Sibs: 9, 10, 60, 68, 77; succession in, 71–72

Skertchly, William: 83, 84, 89, 92, 93

Slave Coast: 106, 164

Slave raids: 11, 20, 22

Slaves: royal, 53; prices of, 112–13, 123

Slave trade: early history of, 17–19; modern, 19, 20; mentioned, 22; bureaucratic obstacles to, 111–12; cost of, 114–115; monopoly of, 115

Slave wars: 135

Smithies: 46–47

Smiths: 89–90

Snelgrave, William: 30, 34, 37

So (craft guilds): xxii, 61, 65, 66

Sodudo (Market women's organizations): 56, 87–88

Songhai: 10, 191

Sortings: 148–68; definition of, 149–50; sample of, 152

Statecraft: xix

Sugar cane: 17, 21

Supply and demand: xiv, xxi

Taxes: collection of, 44–45; cattle, 45; on salt, 45; on iron, 46–47; on internal trade, 47; on agricultural products, 48; inheritance, 48; poll, 48; in kind, 48; burial, 48–49

Technology: xvi

Togo: 11

Topko (Minister of Agriculture): 38

Tori: 114

Towrson, William: 146

Trade: definition of, xvi; administered, xvii, 141, 174; mentioned, xxi; neighborhood, xxii; distinguished from market, 94–95; silent, 99; goods, native and European, 143; English and French agreements on, 161–62

Traders: Arab, 180–81

Tribute: Dahomean, 24

Wage labor: 50–51

Weavers: 88–89

"Weight of the measure": 146–48, 149

Wemenou: 24

Whydah: ix, xxiii, 8, 21, 24, 26, 27, 30, 35, 82, 101, 106, 109, Chapter 7, pp. 99–125; offered to the English, 30; neutrality of, 129–30; Dahomean takeover of, 131–37

Wilmot, Commander: 49

Work parties: 65

Wyndham, H. A.: 142

Yavogan (Dahomean Viceroy): 136, 150, 166

Yoruba: 10

The Royal Palace and th

From Père J. B. Labat, *Voyage du Chevalier des Marchais en Guinée . . . en 1725, 1726, 172*